Becoming Reflective Students and Teachers

With Portfolios and Authentic Assessment

PSYCHOLOGY IN THE CLASSROOM: A SERIES ON APPLIED EDUCATIONAL PSYCHOLOGY

A collaborative project of APA Division 15 (Educational Psychology) and APA Books.

Barbara L. McCombs and Sharon McNeely, Series Editors

Series Titles

*Becoming Reflective Students and Teachers With Portfolios
    and Authentic Assessment*—Paris & Ayres
Motivating Hard to Reach Students—McCombs & Pope
*New Approaches to Literacy: Helping Students Develop Reading
    and Writing Skills*—Marzano & Paynter

In Preparation

Professional Development and Teachers as Problem Solvers—
    Berliner & Belshé
Building Home/School Relationships—Stiller & Turner
Designing Integrated Curricula—Jones, Rasmussen, & Lindberg
Effective Learning and Study Strategies—Weinstein & Hume
Positive Affective Climates—Mills & Timm
Positive Classroom Structures and Discipline—Ridley & Walther
Reducing Test Anxiety and Boredom—Tobias & Tobias

Becoming Reflective Students and Teachers

With Portfolios and Authentic Assessment

Scott G. Paris and Linda R. Ayres

AMERICAN PSYCHOLOGICAL ASSOCIATION | WASHINGTON, DC

Published by
American Psychological Association
750 First Street, NE
Washington, DC 20002

Copies may be ordered from
APA Order Department
P.O. Box 2710
Hyattsville, MD 20784

In the UK and Europe, copies may be ordered from
American Psychological Association
3 Henrietta Street
Covent Garden, London
WC2E 8LU England

Typeset in Berkeley and Arbitrary Sans by KINETIK Communication Graphics, Inc., Washington, DC

Printer: Data Reproductions Corp., Rochester Hills, MI
Cover and Text Designer: KINETIK Communication Graphics, Inc., Washington, DC
Technical/Production Editor: Olin J. Nettles

Library of Congress Cataloging-in-Publication Data
Paris, Scott G.
    Becoming reflective students and teachers with portfolios and authentic assessment / Scott G. Paris and Linda R. Ayres.
    p.   cm. — (Psychology in the classroom)
    Includes bibliographical references
    ISBN 1-55798-252-X (acid-free paper)
    1. Portfolios in education. 2. Language arts (Elementary)
3. Education, Elementary–Parent participation. 4. Students—
Self-rating of. I. Ayres, Linda R. II. Title. III. Series.
LB1029.P67P37 1994
371.2'6—dc20   94-12481
                                                                    CIP

British Library Cataloguing-in-Publication Data
A CIP record is available from the British Library.

Printed in the United States of America
First Edition

We dedicate this book to our mothers, Muriel Paris and Georgia Ricker, our first teachers. Their dedication to teaching others has touched the lives of countless children and their families. They showed by example how to combine high expectations, concern for their students' well-being, and professional commitment while raising a family. We grew as teachers from the models they provided us, and we treasure the lasting lessons we learned from them.

TABLE OF CONTENTS

PREFACE

As we reflect on our own notions about learning and development, we are struck with the dramatic changes in our understanding over the years. Twenty years ago, when we began to teach college students and young children, respectively, we both considered instruction something that teachers delivered, and we viewed the content from a cognitive perspective. Our jobs were to help students acquire knowledge by making the information meaningful, by providing background knowledge and experience as schemata, and by provoking inferential and critical thinking. As teachers, we were concerned with the textbooks, the organization of our curricula, and the logical and sequential aspects of information and exercises. We tried to motivate students with our enthusiasm and interesting presentations as we led them through the mazes of requirements that had been erected to ensure their learning. We did not invent projects, journals, and self-reflection activities for students then, nor did we understand the concept of self-regulated learning as an overarching classroom objective. Maybe we were just novices, maybe it was our own education in the 1960s, or maybe it was the cognitive focus of education in the 1970s. We look back on the changes in our practices and views, proud of what we did then but excited about the new practices that we have learned, and wonder if other teachers who have changed their practices share the same mixed reactions of amusement, satisfaction, amazement, and pride.

We hope this book motivates teachers and parents to reflect on their own ideas about education and to encourage greater self-assessment in their children through deeper engagement with meaningful learning in classrooms. We describe a rich variety of possible activities to provoke students' review of their work, analyses of their motivation, appraisal of their learning strategies, and collaboration with others. The teachers in our projects were bold enough to try new assessment practices, and we encourage others to take the same calculated risks and make the same enduring investments. Choose a few activities that fit your students and teaching styles. Fit them into the overall, annual assessment program, and align them with the daily curriculum. Start small, think big, and talk with a partner as you experiment with new approaches. In our projects, teachers introduced portfolios to students in the first week of class, explained them to parents at the first Parents' Night, and maintained their systems throughout the year. They had a plan to weave assessment activities into their instruction, and they stuck with it.

We realize that some teachers' plans were aimed at "collecting student portfolios," whereas other teachers had less procedural goals that were aimed at promoting "shared responsibility for learning." Yet most of the plans worked. The payoffs came from the students (and parents) who understood how the activities in the portfolios fostered learning and literacy. Their new understanding showed in their increased enthusiasm and thoughtfulness for learning. Research and theories are seldom as convincing to teachers as the reactions in their students, so we designed our project as a "learn-as-you-go" system. The difficulty of educational reform is analogous to repairing your car while you are traveling at 60 mph down the highway. Teachers are faced with the task of experimenting with new forms of assessment while simultaneously becoming familiar with new books, materials, classrooms, staffs, children, and parents. It is an impossible task to do alone without a coherent vision of where you want to go.

> I am not a teacher; only a fellow traveler of whom you asked the way. I pointed ahead—ahead of myself as well as you. George Bernard Shaw

This book tells success stories of teachers who implemented literacy portfolios in their classrooms and observed many positive consequences. We hope that the excitement of teachers, the appreciation of parents, and the insights of students that we have gathered in this book stimulate readers to reflect on their own experiences as teachers and learners. We tried to capture compelling examples of teachers and students working together and their heart-warming vignettes to illustrate the power that new approaches to assessment can have on the psychological dynamics in classrooms. These rich and varied activities, albeit drawn only from literacy portfolios, provide tangible models of the many exciting forms of assessment and learning that we have seen. This book charts a course for new directions of assessment and new destinations for students. We provide clear signposts to guide the journeys and provisions to sustain the travelers as they follow their developmental pathways.

We believe that the bridges from theory to practice must include specific and effective activities that teachers can adapt, not just copy, in their own classrooms to foster students' involvement in assessing their own learning. The examples of conferences, journals, and portfolios offer practical tools for teachers, but each one must be tailored to fit the needs and backgrounds of particular students. We are striving to provide effective models for teachers, to instill positive goals in our students, and to paint attainable visions for educators and parents. We have been energized by the accomplishments of our students and colleagues who have become more self-regulated learners and teachers. We hope that their insights and enthusiasm will be contagious.

ACKNOWLEDGMENTS

We extend our thanks to the teachers and administrators in the Ann Arbor Public School District and the Walled Lake Consolidated School District for their enthusiastic participation in our portfolio projects. We learned a great deal about effective classrooms from our experiences with teachers and students, and their accomplishments and motivation lifted our spirits on many occasions. We are especially grateful to three teachers, Jeanie Brown, Barb Fiorini, and Lynn Mangold, who gave freely of their time to discuss classroom practices, student learning, and teaching philosophies. The examples and reflections from classroom practice are rich because these teachers were willing to share their perspectives on their own professional development. Although we have changed the names in this book to preserve anonymity of the teachers and schools, we gratefully acknowledge the time, energy, and insights provided by many teachers, including Judy Braun, Cynthia Caviani, Gail Davidson, Linda Davis, Chris Fogle, Nancy Fraunheim, Sally Freeman, Susan Friday, Marge Grams, Lori Greene, Judy Groninger, Maureen Haldane, Joane Hertler, Wanda Huber, Dorothy Gustafson, Jean Kelsey, Sally Keeney, Laurel Kibilowski, Bob Marijanovich, Roxane Mellema, Jan Sofran, Gayle Weakland, and Tom Yeager.

introduction

A Vibrant Classroom

"The purpose of education is to allow each individual to come into full possession of his or her personal power." John Dewey

It is the first week of June in Joanie Moore's third-grade classroom in Michigan. Summer vacation is around the corner and children are brimming with excitement. It is not just the "end of the year" excitement that is apparent in children's faces; they are excited because of the work they are doing. They are finishing projects, books, and portfolios that they have worked on all year. In the back corner, Joanie sits with

8-year-old Amy as they review various pieces of work in her portfolio. Around the room, other students are working, some individually and some in groups, on what seem to be loosely related activities that make up the language arts time block in Joanie's room.

Joanie and Amy are sifting through different pieces of work that Amy has put in her portfolio. She has included her book log, for example, which indicates the number of books that she read during the spring, and she is looking back at her other book logs to see how many books she read during the entire year. Joanie uses reading packets that include self-evaluations by each child, which Amy has also included in her portfolio. Together, they review the kinds of things that Amy has read, both the genre and difficulty, as well as Amy's evaluations of her reading performance. As they review, compare, and discuss the different pieces of work, Joanie records comments on a summary sheet that she completes every grading period. This is part of Amy's permanent portfolio record and will go on to next year's teacher, so Amy is eager to read it and add her comments as well.

Meanwhile, Joe is also reviewing his portfolio to decide what to take to his parents for his Home Portfolio. Early in the year, Joanie established the Home Portfolios, like other teachers in her district, as a way of showing parents the kinds of daily work that their children produce. Parents were encouraged to create a place to store these materials so that the students' Home Portfolios look very much like their School Portfolios. These two portfolios are linked together conceptually and functionally; they allow students to carry things back and forth and keep the work they value. The parents of Joanie's students were kept informed of their children's progress as they created these archival records of their children's achievements. Because of the parents' familiarity with their children's work, the parent–teacher conferences were informative and valuable for all participants. The conferences often focused on these work samples, which provided clear indications of progress that children had made.

Nearby, Meaghan and Kristin are sitting on the floor in the book corner reading *How to Eat Fried Worms* and taking turns summarizing their reactions to the text. In between occasional giggles and corrections, they take notes about the characters, setting, and plot as they begin to plan how they will write their reports later. Not far away, Charlie is busy writing a letter to next year's teacher as part of his annual review. He has made a chart indicating his academic strengths and interests and is now composing a letter to communicate these bits of information to his future fourth-grade teacher.

> In an integrated language arts classroom, children seek and construct meaning as they read, write, and discuss ideas in authentic contexts.

In the middle of the room is a team of four students putting the last touches on a report about living in Michigan during the 1800s based on their recent field trip to Greenfield Village. They focused on different aspects of pioneer life as they toured the 19th-century community. They merged their separate notes into one joint report that is almost complete. Another team of three children is not far away, working on a mystery that they will read to the class from the "Author's Chair," one of the ways that the teacher has legitimized the status of every student as an author. They have used diagrams and webs to organize their ideas about the text structure, and now they are brainstorming about the plot before they begin to write the text. Both of these groups enjoy working in teams. Joanie has provided many opportunities for students to work together, because she knows the advantages of cooperative learning.

Other children are scattered throughout the room, engaged in various reading and writing activities as well. Andy is hard at work at the computer, revising one of his stories for a final draft that he will soon print and bind in his own book. It will join the collection of other students' original published works before they are taken home for the summer. Anthony is at a table with a parent who has come in to help children edit and revise their writing. In this conference, Anthony is correcting his spelling and grammar on the letter he has written to next year's teacher. Joanie moves around the room, sometimes just observing and sometimes offering advice, to assure that all students are making progress on their tasks.

CREATING MOTIVATING CLASSROOMS

Is this a remarkable class? Not for Joanie and countless teachers like her. This is the daily morning hubbub of children working independently and together as they discover the excitement of learning and expressing new ideas with each other. It is active, noisy, and apparently unsupervised, but goal-directed for each of the students. This is an integrated language arts classroom in which reading, writing, speaking, and listening are experienced for meaningful purposes. Joanie's students display genuine effort and persistence in each of these tasks because they find the activities challenging and motivating. As they move to different areas of the curriculum, children's projects and partners may change, but their intrinsic motivation and inquiry-based learning are evident all day long.

CHARACTERISTICS OF STUDENT-CENTERED CLASSROOMS

- Authentic projects
- Learning centers
- Flexible groups and partners
- Response journals and thinking logs
- Student–teacher conferences
- Hands-on materials and technology
- Caring atmosphere
- Exhibitions of students' work
- Classroom libraries
- Peer discussions and tutoring

What do we notice about the students? There is a buzzing of busy minds as students move around the classroom. They are not sitting in desks listening to the teacher or doing the same task very often. Instead, they are working independently or in small groups on different activities. Older students or adults are often present to help students find and discuss information. The curriculum is not dictated by rigid time periods or marching through prescribed materials. Students search for information and use classroom libraries, materials, and other people as resources for learning. The tasks are given by teachers, but they are deliberately open-ended to encourage students to construct their own meaning from the materials they read and write. This encourages students to take initiative, to monitor their time, and to direct their own learning.

What do we notice about the teacher? During this morning's language arts block, she is certainly not the center of attention. Instead, she moves from student to student, working individually with students or groups. In order to have daily conferences, she spends part of her morning quietly talking with individual students for 5 to 15 minutes at a time in the corner as they review their portfolios. Her energy is not all directed toward behavioral control or classroom management, because students are motivated by the projects, themes, and teams that permeate her classroom. They are required to be independent learners who search for information, monitor each others' performance, and work together for legitimate purposes.

Joanie often acts as a consultant or a coach to her students, providing periodic reminders or hints to help students accomplish their tasks. Sometimes she acts as a facilitator, whereas at other times she acts as a director. On some occasions, you might see her providing direct instruction to the whole class about reading or writing strategies, earth science, or place value borrowing. She maintains a constant sense of excitement and commitment among her students by mixing a variety of whole-class instruction with independent learning, cooperative

> Students display initiative and responsibility when activities are open-ended and stimulating.

teamwork, and flexible grouping. Joanie does not organize her day by worksheets or clock periods. Instead, she organizes activities around questions and projects that fit the needs and interests of her students. She poses problems to her students and encourages them to search for solutions. Learning is a dynamic process in Joanie's classroom—and so is assessment.

In case you did not notice, in this vignette of a third-grade classroom, nearly all of the learning activities are also used for assessment. Whether the task is writing a letter, polishing a final draft, brainstorming a story structure, or reading with partners, every activity provides an opportunity for assessment of the content of children's knowledge as well as their processes of learning. Because Joanie wants these opportunities for learning and assessment to be mutually informative, they are interwoven in daily activities. Some of the assessment is done informally through observation and anecdotal notes, but other assessments are conducted by students themselves. Joanie regularly asks students to evaluate their own performance and progress, which provides her with valuable information about each child. Periodically, she meets with students in conferences or provides them with surveys or inventories to probe their understanding. These assessments are designed to provide personalized profiles of each student from a variety of evidence (Valencia, 1990).

> Every learning activity provides an opportunity for assessment of the content of children's knowledge, as well as their processes of learning.

Indeed, the students themselves are critical contributors to the assessment process and are not simply the respondents to a series of tests. Joanie believes that 8- and 9-year-olds should be encouraged to reflect on their own learning, to consider their strengths and weaknesses, to set purposes and goals, to provide help to others, and to feel pride in their accomplishments. These are reflective students who are flourishing in a classroom led by a reflective teacher. Joanie models self-evaluation, persistence, revision, and optimism about progress on her own behavior. Just as she is reflective about the tasks that she provides to students, her students are reflective about what and how they learn.

FEATURES OF AUTHENTIC ASSESSMENT

Our examples of third grade students engaged in assessing their performance as they learn are intended to illustrate authentic assessment practices in action. We have deliberately chosen to show by example what authentic assessment looks like, because a simple definition does not capture the interpersonal dynamics and power of authentic assessment. Furthermore, we know that what is "authentic" in one school or in one state may not be authentic in other schools or states. Why? Because authentic assessment is defined by the situational appropriateness of teaching and learning practices. The task of all teachers is to make sure that assessment in their classrooms reflects the valued outcomes in their curricula and is aligned with their instructional methods so that students regard the assessments as genuine and fair. Despite the difficulties in defining authentic assessment in a single manner, it is important to identify some of the principles that underlie this approach. Valencia, Hiebert, and Afflerbach (1994) provided extended discussions and additional classroom examples of authentic assessment that embody the following features:

> Students need to be active participants in assessment of their own learning rather than passive respondents to a series of tests.

1. Authentic assessment is consistent with classroom practices. It has instructional and curricular validity because assessment procedures and content are derived from students' everyday learning in school. In practice, this means that students are asked questions about meaningful information and asked to solve problems that are relevant to their educational experiences.

2. Authentic assessment collects diverse evidence of students' learning from multiple activities. Rather than relying on single tests or narrow samples of students' knowl-

edge, authentic assessment involves gathering evidence over time from many different academic activities (Calfee & Hiebert, 1990). These performance measures might include oral readings and retellings, multiple-choice tests about text, written responses to literature, creative writing, book logs, and journals (Winograd, Paris, & Bridge, 1991).

3. Authentic assessment promotes learning and teaching among the participants. Assessment is functional, pragmatic, and beneficial. Messick (1989) argues that validity ought to include an account of the consequences of assessment so that it results in the intended effects and has no unintended consequences (cf. Linn, Baker, & Dunbar, 1991). Thus, authentic assessment seeks to promote students' learning and motivation directly and is evaluated against that benchmark.

4. Authentic assessment reflects local values, standards, and control. It is not imposed externally with norms and expectations from an unknown population, nor are control and authority removed from the participants. Authentic assessment can be modified by teachers to elicit optimal performance from students and provide useful information to parents and administrators. What is measured is valued in the community, and how it is assessed assures that students are providing reliable indicators of their performance.

CONSEQUENCES FOR THE PARTICIPANTS

We want to step back from this illustration of Joanie Moore's third grade to examine how various kinds of classroom activities can encourage teachers and students to become reflective and self-regulated learners. Some of these activities might be classified as assessment, yet their purposes extend beyond diagnostic and summative functions of assessment because they energize learning. The motivational consequences of these activities makes

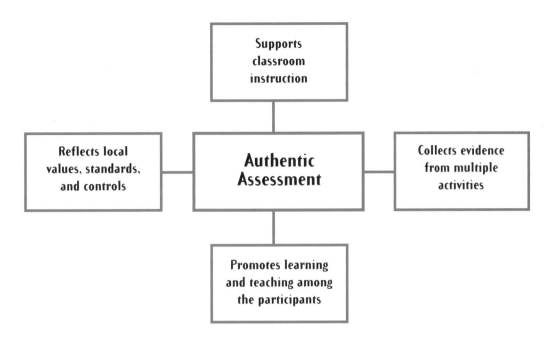

Figure 1: *Features of authentic classroom assessment.*

them "drive" children's learning with both force and purpose. Although standardized achievement tests are sometimes referred to as "high-stakes testing," we believe that activities in the classroom that promote self-regulated learning are more accurately regarded as "high-stakes" because they establish motivational orientations for lifelong learning, and not simply short-term academic goals designed to yield high test scores. The participants in Joanie's class value their daily activities more than occasional test scores because they provide critical information about the effort and quality of their work. Let us briefly consider their perspectives to understand how students, teachers, and parents react to the opportunities to reflect upon both children's learning and teaching practices. We have been impressed by the renewed commitment and responsibility that all three groups of participants display as a consequence of their reflections.

> Assessment becomes "high-stakes" when it establishes priorities for teaching and learning.

Students' Reflections

Students in Joanie's class are actively engaged in managing their own learning because the activities are often open-ended; that is, the procedures for completing the task are not specified exactly by the teacher but driven by the inquiries of the students. It is not chaotic, however, because students understand the teacher's expectations and roles. For example, they understand the writing process and the need to plan, revise, and collaborate; they understand pair-share reading activities; they understand how to use the library; and they know they can receive hints and support from peers and teachers when needed. Students also understand how and why to review their work; they regard self-evaluation as a natural part of their learning. For example, one fifth-grader wrote the following reaction to her portfolio:

> The portfolio has helped me realize my potential as a competent writer by adding more details. I'm more aware of my strengths and my challenges. I'm *not afraid* to try and figure out the answer in a subject I'm not good in.

This brief comment reveals her sense of self-efficacy and how examining her own work has helped her accept challenges. Figure 2 shows how Chris, a third grader, reflected on some of the things he learned during the year. Some of the things he reported were curriculum based ("I learned that there is life on a rotting log."), some things were metacognitive ("I learned that reading expository text is harder than narrative."), and some revealed his understanding of classroom assessment practices ("I learned that a portfolio is something to tell you about your progress and what you need to work on").

The overarching purpose of portfolios is to create a sense of personal ownership over one's accomplishments, because ownership engenders feelings of pride, responsibility, and dedication.

Students can reflect on their performance in many ways. Teachers might provide opportunities for students

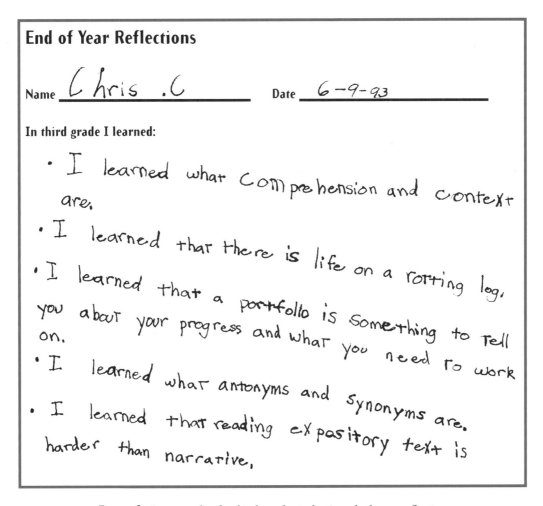

End of Year Reflections

Name __Chris .C__   Date __6-9-93__

In third grade I learned:

- I learned what comprehension and context are.
- I learned that there is life on a rotting log.
- I learned that a portfolio is something to tell you about your progress and what you need to work on.
- I learned what antonyms and synonyms are.
- I learned that reading expository text is harder than narrative.

Figure 2: *An example of a third-grade student's end-of-year reflection.*

to evaluate their own work in checklists or answers to questions; they might encourage peers to work together to provide suggestions for revisions; or they might use journals, autobiographies, or self-portraits in letters to allow students to reflect on themselves as learners. The overarching purpose of these activities is to create a sense of personal ownership over one's accomplishments (cf. Au, Scheu, Kawakami, & Herman, 1990), because ownership engenders feelings of pride, responsibility, and dedication. From a motivational perspective, students adopt mastery goals and intrinsic standards when they feel ownership over their own learning (Covington, 1992; De Charms, 1968). From a metacognitive perspective, students develop insights about their abilities, the tasks they perform, and the strategies that are useful

(Brown, Bransford, Ferrara, & Campione, 1983; Paris & Byrnes, 1989). One consequence of students' reflections on their learning is deeper engagement in schoolwork, which is evident in their effort, persistence, and personal standards.

Teachers' Reflections

Joanie has designed her classroom to meet many goals, some of which are directly related to stimulating students' and parents' reflections. Most teachers use assessment to make instructional decisions about the progress of their students and the need for further instruction. Joanie has created an environment in which she is not the only evaluator and decision maker; her students and their parents share the same roles. This makes her job more *efficient* because it saves time and allows her to consult individually with students as others work independently, and more *effective* because students receive multiple sources of feedback on their performance.

Teachers benefit from opportunities to reflect on their classrooms just as much as students. On several occasions, we asked teachers in our Portfolio Project to review and assess their own practices. For example, early in the school year, we asked teachers to report how they had introduced portfolios in their classrooms, what they liked about them so far, and what they might do differently next year. Dorothy, a first-grade teacher, said,

> I told the children that I would be saving some of their writing so we can see how much they have learned this year. I also mentioned that I would be asking them questions about reading and how they felt about it. I feel that I have started the year out with a much greater focus on writing than ever before. I *really* feel great about what I see in the way of progress in the students. It's a joy! At present we only have a couple of things in their portfolios. The greatest factor, I believe, since the first week and now is the confidence that the children have.

It's OK to try—I can do it! I might make
a mistake but it's all right.

We also asked teachers to reflect on their teaching styles after they had used portfolios for two years in their classrooms, and we were amazed at the changes expressed by teachers. They, like students, had developed insights about what makes their practices effective, and they displayed ownership and pride in their new methods. For example, one teacher compared her old and new ideas about teaching by labeling the two columns "I used to … but now I …." as shown below.

One Teacher's Reflections

I used to …	*But now I …*
view children as just sitting there and partaking of my worthwhile teaching	see them as active, involved learners and my role is more like a facilitator
plan separate lessons for each area of the curriculum	plan holistically and make connections to real-life learning
use the books they gave me, including "scripts" from the Teacher's Edition	pull lessons from a variety of sources
assess children with paper and pencil tests	look at their daily work and assess their thoughts and feelings too
view my principal as an "absolute ruler"	view my principal as a colleague
like children, but I taught "material"	feel like teaching is a "calling" to get students involved in their own learning

Another teacher said, " I used to provide everything for my kids, but now I enlist the students to find materials and become involved in their own preparation. Thus, the doer is the learner." She also said, "I used to view my colleagues as helpful in sharing materials, but now I seek their views and advice to help students connect information at their grade level."

Reflections about teaching and colleagues may alter what teachers do in classrooms, but reflections on interpersonal relationships also elicit powerful emotional reactions. Here is a first-grade teacher's reflections, at the end of a school year, on her relationships with her students and their parents:

> Interviewer: How about your relationship with your students—do you respond to them differently now than you used to?
>
> Liz: Yeah, I feel a much closer relationship to them. I was very sad to see this year's class go—I felt we had a terrific year. I've been teaching 19 years and I cried—and they cried—we all hugged each other. I feel that when you learn this way, it's very up-front and personal, and ...
>
> Interviewer: Why do you think it's like that? What's happening now that didn't happen before?
>
> Liz: I think, for one thing, because I want to be a model as a lifelong learner, I'm sharing more of my own personal learning experiences ... my writing with them, my reading with them, ... (I show them) how I choose books, how I choose topics to write, why I choose to take certain classes on my own because I'm a learner too, and they're surprised at all of this—they're surprised that their teacher has a life outside of the classroom! And they start viewing you a little bit different. And I think that opens *them* up to start sharing things about themselves that they might not normally share ....

We have seen similar reactions among other teachers who are amazed how their students respond in their classrooms when they establish a climate of mutual respect, emotional safety, and shared responsibility. This does not happen because of annual "self-esteem" days or superficial attention to students' feelings. Instead, we believe that daily attention to activities that engage students in their own learning and self-appraisal are critical for enhancing intrinsic motivation. Students need to become familiar and comfortable with self-assessment through repeated activities, and teachers need to realize that this is part of a long developmental process. This is part of the "apprenticeship" of students, a model of teaching and learning that emphasizes how participation of students moves from the periphery to the center of activities as they acquire the skills and knowledge to regulate their own learning (Lave & Wegner, 1991; Rogoff, 1990). Teachers recognize the impact of students' reflections when teachers review what works for their students, because portfolios foster insights in students and teachers in a parallel fashion. Their reactions are just a few samples of the power of teachers' reflections to influence their classroom practices.

Parents' Reflections

Parents want to know what their children are learning and how they are progressing. Traditional test scores alone are not adequate to meet their needs, so Joanie has developed several procedures to keep parents informed and involved in their children's education. One tactic is to send a form letter home to parents along with some of the child's portfolio materials. The letter simply asks parents to review their children's work together, sign the form, and return it to school. Many parents take the opportunity to write notes to teachers on the forms, such as the responses below:

> Dear Mrs. Moore,
>
> Yes, we reviewed Shannon's portfolio. I will save it. I wish all teachers had your teaching method, with progress reports, papers to sign, and an end-of-year conference. It makes the parents keep up and in touch with their child's school work and progress. I know

Shannon worked hard this year and it shows. I am so glad she had you for a teacher. We will miss you next year.

Sincerely,
The W. Family
Rob, Susan, Michelle,
Tyler, Candace, Baby Sean

Dear Mrs. Moore,

I think that the portfolio is a wonderful idea! It's nice to be able to see the progress this year and then have something to save.

Diane S.

Dear Mrs. Moore,

I saw a variety of reading, spelling, math work. I thank you for your way, which is the best way of teaching, and how you organized these papers so I can keep it for his records.

Amit G.

Parents often have strong desires to be involved in their children's education but few opportunities to share their experiences. Letters, conferences, and portfolio reviews can all help parents to understand teachers' practices and to reflect on their children's learning. Why is this important? One reason is that parents often gauge their children's education against their own experiences and find it difficult to understand instruction and assessment practices when they are considerably different from what parents did 20 or 30 years before. For example, some parents become agitated by teachers' acceptance of invented spelling in first grade, others want more math drills, and other parents are perplexed by the lack of lecturing in the middle grades. However, when parents can reflect on school practices through activities with their children or through communication with teachers, they become partners with teachers. How?

> When parents can reflect upon school practices through activities with their children or through communication with teachers, they become supportive partners.

First, they develop better understanding of the reasons for various classroom practices, because they see their children's performance firsthand. Second, parents know what they can do to support school activities with appropriate practices at home. This has a direct impact on teachers. Consider the following excerpts from an interview with a teacher about parental involvement in the children's education.

Interviewer: Well, how about the parents? Let's talk a little bit more about your relationships with them. Since you've been working with more of a child-centered approach, do you feel like your relationships with the parents have been enhanced?

Rosie: Yes, I think they have [improved]. I think if you don't communicate with the parents, they get scared because all they know is how they went to school with workbooks and sitting in their seats, and they come into my room—there are no desks, there are tables, there's stuff all over the room, stuff's hanging everywhere—there are projects on every possible place you could have …. Especially second-semester first grade, when they can really start to take off. I mean, it just doesn't look like what school used to look like. And unless you take the time to educate them, get them involved in your classroom, to come in and help out with the centers, they don't understand why and what you're doing.

Interviewer: When you meet with the parents at conference time, do the portfolios help you?

Rosie: Oh, it made conferences absolutely wonderful. When I was done sharing all the things, the parents were just …, their mouths were hanging open. They said, "I never *knew* this is what went on in first grade! Oh my goodness! This is a *tremendous* amount of learning." And I don't think they would have understood that unless we had the portfolio as a guide to walk them through .... I told the parents at any time, I'd be willing to meet with them, and some of them took advantage of that and did come in.

Interviewer: They know what's going on in your classroom. So you think that there's a change in your relationship with parents ....

Rosie: I think it's more open. I think it's much more open—there's a lot more communication going on than there was before. I think parents just ... before, accepted, "OK, this is the way we went to school, this is the way it's done ...." And now it's new and they're realizing what the interactive nature is and *they* become more interactive with you. And they feel that *I* know their child better and I really do know their child. When I would point out certain things and they would say, "I can't believe you *know* that ...." Knows them by name, knows their interests, their likes, their cares, their concerns. And when I would share their writing with them, which is *so* personal for students, tears were in parents' eyes at some of the wonderful things that children had written.

Partnerships begin with common goals and understandings. In some classrooms, teachers create activities that bring students, teachers, and parents together. Thus, reflection can help parents understand what and how their children are learning. Activities such as portfolios provide common knowledge and emotional bridges between home and school that help prepare parents for different roles and responsibilities so that they can create motivating environments for learning that stretch beyond school.

OVERVIEW OF THIS BOOK

This book is written for teachers and parents who help children to develop insights into their own learning, to reflect on their efforts and achievements, and to take responsibility for their educational success. Many of the examples are taken from literacy activities in K–6 classrooms, but the principles can be extended easily to older students who are learning to assess their own progress across multiple types of curricula. Indeed, teachers and students modified their portfolios throughout the year to accommodate the rest of the curricula by adding projects, worksheets, journals, and other artifacts that they produced. The ingenuity of the teachers is refreshing, and the spontaneity and ease with which they transformed literacy portfolios into portfolios for their entire curricula are reassuring to us. The system we introduced empowers and enables teachers to make assessment authentic in their own classrooms.

> Portfolios provide common knowledge and emotional bridges between home and school.

Our ideas about the value of partnerships and reflections are derived from our own experiences with teachers and children. We have collaborated as reflective partners to create this book and the portfolio assessment project described in it and have worked with our colleagues in schools with the same objectives, to learn from each other and to grow as professionals together. We hope the ideas in the book are useful to graduate students in literacy and education programs and relevant to the daily experiences of K–12 classroom teachers. The book might be used for self-study, for professional development workshops, or as a guide for school personnel who are working to establish authentic assessment procedures in classrooms.

If the opening vignette has whetted your appetite for more illustrations of how teachers can promote motivated, reflective students, we invite you to continue reading. The first goal in this book is to provide a conceptual foundation for authentic assessment in a child-centered curriculum that supports the growth of self-regulated learning. The second goal is to describe how learner-centered assessment stimulates students to monitor and assess their own progress and accomplishments in school. The third goal is to show how teachers use portfolios, journals, self-assessments, and conferences to promote reflections. The fourth goal is to describe how portfolios allow teachers and parents to communicate more effectively about children's academic progress so that teachers can enlist the involvement of parents as coteachers. The fifth goal is to illustrate how the same principles of self-assessment that help students also permit teachers to reflect on their own practices and professional development.

The themes of becoming more insightful through reflecting and sharing permeate the book and apply to children, teachers, and parents. This will be evident in the self-directed activities and suggested readings at the end of each chapter that are designed to make these principles tangible. The activities are divided into four sections—reflecting, responding, sharing, and reviewing—so that readers can react to the ideas and apply them to their own educational settings. We believe deeply that schools can be exciting places for teachers, students, and parents to work and learn together and that authentic assessment is fundamental to the partnerships required for educational reform and success.

STATEMENT OF RATIONALE AND GOALS

Rationale

Testing is no longer an adequate measure of students' learning nor a sufficient reason for students to invest effort in schoolwork. New methods of assessment that provide multidimensional and longitudinal portraits of students' strengths and weaknesses are required to provide developmental benchmarks of learning. These new forms of assessment provide longitudinal evidence and personal stories of individuals' learning and development, not just snapshots of test scores, grades, and comments on report cards. Authentic assessments allow students to participate actively in their own learning, and provide opportunities for teachers to align their curriculum, instruction, and assessment practices. When teachers, students, and parents work together to use assessments as tools for enhancing learning, all participants are more informed and motivated to achieve high standards of success.

Goals for the Readers of this Book

1. To understand how students' self-regulated learning is enhanced by learner-centered assessment practices.

2. To understand the kinds of activities that teachers can provide across the curricula to promote students' self-assessment of their own learning.

3. To understand how teachers and parents can connect learning experiences at home and school with authentic assessment.

4. To understand how teachers can increase their professional skills by reflecting on their own assessment practices and sharing information with other teachers.

5. To understand that children's strategic, motivated, and adventurous approaches to learning can be nurtured every day by teachers and parents who provide meaningful opportunities for children to be involved in assessing and directing their own learning.

1 **Reflecting**: Think about a really exciting, memorable experience you had as a student—anytime from elementary school through college. Imagine yourself in that classroom again and describe what made it exciting for you. Write down some of the key words, events, and feelings that come to your mind as you reminisce.

2 **Responding:** Think about the changes in your own teaching (or parenting) practices over the years, and the reasons for the changes, as you fill out the chart below.

I used to …	But I realized …	So now I …	Because …

3 **Sharing:** Share your reflections about exciting classrooms with a fellow teacher or a relative. Compare the characteristics of their experiences to your own reflections to see the similarities across schools that may differ widely in location, time, and structure.

4 **Reviewing:** Look back in this chapter at the list of features of student-centered classrooms and compare these features to the characteristics of an exciting classroom that you recalled. Many of them might be similar because we often remember teachers who were caring, assignments that allowed us to explore our personal interests, friends who helped us learn, and activities that made us feel proud of our hard work and good ideas. It is often easy for teachers to identify such underlying principles of classrooms that stimulate students' motivation and learning when they are given opportunities to reflect on their own experiences and successes. For this reason, time for reflection is important. Teachers can also learn about student-centered classrooms and self-regulated learning through professional development workshops and ideas presented in journals, books, and conferences. It is important for districts to provide both time and a coherent vision for change if teachers are expected to try new approaches. Then, these insights need to be shared among teachers to foster conversations about new approaches to learning, instruction, and assessment.

SUGGESTED READINGS

Brooks, J. G., & Brooks, M. G. (1993). *The case for constructivist classrooms*. Alexandria, VA: Association for Supervision and Curriculum Development.

Glazer, S. M., & Brown, C. S. (1993). *Portfolios and beyond: Collaborative assessment in reading and writing.* Norwood, MA: Christopher-Gordon Publishers.

Valencia, S. W., Hiebert, E. H., & Afflerbach, P. P. (1994). *Authentic reading assessment: Practices and possibilities.* Newark, DE: International Reading Association.

goal one

Understanding Self-Regulated
Learning

"A teacher who is attempting to teach without inspiring the pupil with the desire to learn is hammering on cold iron."

Horace Mann

Joanie Moore's third grade is an exciting classroom with many positive features. We have chosen to highlight a few of the activities and characteristics because they exemplify students' independence and self-regulated learning. What exactly is self-regulated learning and why is it important? What classroom activities motivate children to be inquisitive and independent? What are the psychological dynamics of teaching and learning that we can identify and implement in other classrooms? We address these kinds of questions in this section as we identify principles of learning, teaching, and assessment that are evident in classrooms like Joanie Moore's.

CHARACTERISTICS OF SELF-REGULATED LEARNING

Self-regulated learning describes the motivated and strategic efforts of students to accomplish specific purposes. In our view, it is functional, personal, and independent, precisely the kind of curious knowledge seeking and strategic problem solving that educators value as critical thinking and thoughtfulness. Zimmerman (1989) said that "students can be described as self-regulated to the degree that they are metacognitively, motivationally, and behaviorally active participants in their own learning process" (p.4). He discussed three processes relevant to children's self-assessment: self-observation, self-judgment, and self-reaction. What is missing from this analysis, however, is the purpose, direction, and force of the person's effort, the motivation and reasons for engaging in learning activities. Paris and Cross (1983) described the essence of self-regulated learning as the integration of cognition, motivation, and affect—in other words, the "fusing of skill and will"—as students examine their learning before, during, and after task engagement. We will briefly consider seven features of the motivational and cognitive dynamics that are evident when students direct their own learning.

> Students are self-regulated when they are active participants in their own learning.

First, students select goals to pursue and work on a variety of tasks. This means they have *choices* to consider and autonomy to select different purposes. The work is not compartmentalized by worksheets or time blocks, but rather, all students understand that they must complete a variety of tasks and need to plan how to use their time and resources. Furthermore, self-selected goals are governed by curiosity and intrinsic motivation to display one's competence. Research has shown that goals oriented to extrinsic rewards such as grades, tokens, or praise are less meaningful and sustaining than goals oriented toward intrinsic standards of the student, such as mastery, learning, or improving on one's past performance (Ames & Archer, 1988). Self-regulated learners can choose appropriate goals such as mastery, task completion, extrinsic rewards, or social cooperation, depending on the situation. Usually, self-directed learners choose goals for learning that are tied to personal standards and satisfaction.

A second characteristic of self-regulated learning is the need for *challenge*. In Joanie's class, children adjusted the challenge of the tasks they chose. Whether working on a letter, story, report, or computer, each student adjusted the difficulty of the task to be challenging and interesting, yet also within reach. Some students choose to avoid learning by setting goals that are too easy. They achieve "cheap success" with minimal effort, but this is not sustaining or rewarding in the long run. Other students focus on avoiding failure and shame instead of achieving success. They may set goals that are unrealistically high in order to appear virtuous and to avoid criticisms for their failure (Covington, 1992). However, self-regulated learners have expectations for success that are challenging; they push the edge of their own abilities, which allows for a mixture of success and nonsuccess.

"Nonsuccess" is a more appropriate term than failure, because self-regulated learners are "risk takers" who anticipate difficulties, errors, and "failure" in the normal course of acquiring new knowledge and new skills (Clifford, 1991). Self-regulated learners react to failure differently than children who are passive, fearful, or avoidant learners in the classroom. Self-regulated students see development as proceeding with spurts and plateaus, but generally leading to increased confidence with age and experience. They display eagerness, drive, curiosity and initiative, because their expectations are consistent with an optimistic view of their own development and self-determination (Deci, Vallerand, Pelletier, & Ryan, 1991). "Failure" is a temporary setback for these students, not an indictment of their abilities.

Third, self-regulated students know how to use the resources available to them in a classroom; they have *control* of their own learning. They know how to plan, allocate resources, seek help, evaluate their own performance, and revise and correct their own work. Self-regulated learners are aware of their own learning strategies and know how to use them effectively. They are very much self-directed in terms of pursuing their goals for learning and applying appropriate strategies. For example, students who are independent are not reluctant to use the library, ask a friend, or seek help from teachers when they encounter problems they cannot solve independently. Other students, unfortunately, often fear embarrassment because they view help-seeking as an indication of low ability and thus avoid seeking help or using available resources for fear of appearing less able than other students (Newman & Goldin, 1990). However, the climate and organization of classrooms matter. Students are more likely to seek help and to ask questions in small groups and individual activities than in whole-class discussions where the act of seeking assistance is more public and threatening (Meece, Blumenfeld, & Puro, 1989).

Fourth, self-regulated students *collaborate* as they read and write. They may exchange papers for peer editing when they write, or they may discuss what they are reading in pair-share activities or reciprocal teaching arrangements (Palincsar & Brown, 1984). Collaboration serves two functions, encouraging persistence and providing strategic help when necessary. Students provide these cognitive and motivational resources for one another in the same ways that good teachers provide them for students. Indeed, teachers can model effectively

> When students are provided choice, challenge, control, and collaboration in their classrooms, they are motivated intrinsically to learn.

how to collaborate through their own behavior. Choice, challenge, control, and collaboration are critical aspects of intrinsic motivation (Paris & Turner, 1994; Stipek, 1993), and as we shall illustrate, their importance is evident in the reflections of both students and teachers.

A fifth characteristic of self-regulated learning is the focus on *constructing meaning*. Joanie minimized the use of worksheets and procedural tasks in which students work "to get it done" and instead oriented children to make meaning from the things they read, write, and discuss. Some people describe such activities as "authentic learning" or "whole language," but the key to authenticity seems to be a focus on creating, constructing, debating, sharing, and revising the meaning in a literacy activity (Tharp & Gallimore, 1988). Of course, this is easier to do with good books, thoughtful and creative writing assignments, and cooperative learning arrangements. Self-regulated learners can manage their efforts to fill in blanks on worksheets or fill in bubbles on test forms with appropriate strategies if they must, but their autonomy and creativity are more evident on richer tasks that foster comprehension and communication aimed at making and sharing meaning.

A sixth characteristic of self-regulated learning concerns the *consequences of classroom activities*. The consequences of rich activities are personally rewarding to students who can take pride in their efforts and the meaning they construct. Because their success is a reflection of their personal imagination, comprehension, and strategies, as well as their hard work, they enhance their feelings of ownership and efficacy to a much greater degree than is possible with constrained activities such as copying sentences from the board or filling in worksheets. Self-regulated students evaluate and interpret their behavior in ways that promote further effort. Their attributions for success and failure are constructive, not debilitating, because they understand when and how their behavior is due to controllable forces. For example, some students attribute their prob-

> When students complete challenging tasks and communicate their ideas clearly, they feel confident and competent.

lems or poor performance to lack of ability, whereas others attribute learning difficulties to lack of effort. This classic attributional difference has been observed between children labeled "mastery oriented" and "learned helpless" (Dweck & Leggett, 1988). It has also been observed between males and females on some tasks and even between people of different cultures. For example, Asian students and their families are much more likely to view effort as fundamental to success than American students, who often see ability as more important (Stevenson & Stigler, 1992). Self-regulated students are also less likely to blame others for their problems or credit luck for their successes. They understand that strategies and effort lead to success. Their attributions to controllable causes, such as particular strategies or persistence, are fundamental for maintaining their effort and feeling pride in their accomplishments (Weiner, 1992).

A seventh characteristic of self-regulated learning is an overarching focus on awareness and orchestration of learning, on the *metacognitive aspects of learning.* Self-regulated students monitor their own performance and evaluate their progress against established criteria and reasonable standards (McCombs & Marzano, 1990). They know whether they are improving, and they know when their performance is acceptable to their parents, their teacher, and themselves. They engage in self-reflection often and find it informative, not threatening, to talk to other people about their performance and accomplishments. Paris and Winograd (1990) summarized the twin aspects of students' metacognition as self-appraisal and self-management of their own behavior, critical components of self-regulated learning.

> Self-regulated learners are aware of *what* strategies are available to help them; they understand *how* the strategies operate; they understand *when* they should be applied; and they understand *why* they are necessary.

Self-appraisal includes a variety of knowledge about learning strategies. According to Paris, Lipson, and Wixson (1983), this includes three kinds of metacognitive knowledge. First, self-regulated learners have *declar-*

ative knowledge, information about *what* strategies are available to help them, whether their task is writing a letter, composing a story, searching in the library, or rereading a textbook. They understand the kinds of strategies that can be used before, during, and after reading, writing, and arithmetic.

Second, self-regulated learners *understand procedural knowledge* about strategies, that is, *how* strategies operate. Some students have only a superficial understanding of how to apply strategies. For example, 8- and 9-year-old children who do not understand how to skim may simply read the first and last sentences on a page. If they do not know how to revise the conceptual content and presentation of a paper, their revisions may simply involve making the handwriting neat and correcting the spelling of some words. In contrast, self-regulated learners consider how strategies facilitate the expression and construction of meaning, and they understand how to use strategies selectively and effortfully to accomplish their goals.

Third, self-regulated students understand the *conditional knowledge* about strategies, that is, under what circumstances strategies are helpful, *when* they should be applied, and *why* they are necessary. They may understand why study strategies such as note taking, underlining, or summarizing can facilitate later recall. For them, strategies are not routinely applied to any task; instead, they are chosen and applied selectively. Knowing why one's behavior and strategies are effective (or not) is critical for self-improvement.

In addition to knowing these things about useful strategies for learning, self-regulated learners enact their plans; they fuse their motivational orientations with their knowledge, strategies, and intentions. They know how to make appropriate plans and choose strategies before they begin a task. They know that during a task they should periodically check their performance and possibly revise their strategies. Following task completion, self-regulated students review their work, evaluate their performance, and share their work with others. They also know *volitional strategies* for maintaining their commitment to chosen goals and preventing distractions (Corno, 1992). They are persistent, strategic, and directed in their efforts. That is why self-regulated learning involves motivated problem solving and not simply the exercise of skills or compliance with someone else's directions.

LEARNER-CENTERED PSYCHOLOGICAL PRINCIPLES

We believe that self-regulated learning is encouraged by instructional and assessment practices that promote active engagement of students in their own learning through reflection and review on a daily basis. Our suggestions about assessments that promote self-reflection and self-regulated learning are thus part of the larger context of instruction that is sensitive to the needs and talents of students. A guiding principle in this larger context is that students seek to make sense of the information they receive in classrooms, "to go beyond the information given" (Bruner, 1961), in order to construct schemata of themselves, their peers, their teachers, and the work they perform.

We believe that teachers cannot create challenging classrooms unless they understand—deeply and coherently—the psychological principles of learning and development that they must assess and foster in their students. Otherwise, teachers rely on manuals, textbooks, workbooks, and tests prescribed by others to define and structure their teaching. This is how teachers become managers of materials, classroom disciplinarians, and didactic direction-givers instead of reflective mentors in their classrooms. We hope that teachers take control of their instructional and assessment practices, through knowledge and reflection, in order to create exciting environments that promote children's self-regulated learning.

Assessment must be guided by principles of learning and development, not routine testing prescribed by manuals and mandates.

In 1993, The American Psychological Association formed a Presidential Task Force on Psychology in Education that identified twelve fundamental principles of learner-centered education. We believe that they are also relevant to self-regulated learning and educational reforms of assessment. In the Preamble of the report, the importance of the twelve principles is stated sharply: "educational reform efforts that do not take these principles into account will surely fail." We will briefly paraphrase the principles before describing some parallel learner-centered principles for classroom assessment. Together, these principles about learning and assessment that focus on students provide the practical rationales and conceptual connections for integrating instructional activities, assessment, and self-reflection. A learner-centered focus is critical for improving classroom motivation and learning because these goals are not fostered by attention to test scores, school problems, or the problems of business productivity, the typical foci of media and politicians who propose a variety of school reforms that do not enhance the psychological climate of schools. The entire list of the Task Force's recommended principles, along with the implications for learning and instruction, are included in the appendix.

HOW TRADITIONAL PRACTICES UNDERMINE SELF-REGULATED LEARNING

These lofty principles may strike some as obvious and some as largely rhetorical, the kind of statements that pepper school mission statements, school boards' pledges, and sales brochures for textbooks. Why would a presidential task force find it necessary to make these principles explicit? We believe that education is searching, perhaps desperately and with too many accusations, for new ground, a new springboard for "systemic reform," one of the most recent clarion slogans. Psychology has much to offer those who search for bedrock in the principles of development, teaching, and learning. Since John Dewey's pioneering work on the child-centered approach to education, psychologists have contributed to theories and methods of teaching. Not all of these proposals have been successful, nor are they unanimously endorsed, but there has been remarkable longevity to the ideas of the "progressive school,"

LEARNER-CENTERED PSYCHOLOGICAL PRINCIPLES

1. Learning is an active process of constructing meaning according to the unique experiences of each individual.

2. Students seek to create meaningful and coherent representations of knowledge.

3. Students link new information with existing knowledge in meaningful ways.

4. Strategies for "thinking about thinking" help students to think creatively and critically.

5. What and how much students learn and remember is influenced by their beliefs, goals, expectations, affect, and motivation.

6. Students are naturally curious and enjoy learning, but intense negative emotions and worry thwart enthusiasm.

7. Critical and creative thinking are stimulated by learning tasks that are relevant, authentic, and challenging for each student.

8. Individuals develop physically, intellectually, emotionally and socially in unique ways.

9. Learning is facilitated by social interactions and communication with others in a variety of diverse settings.

10. Self-esteem and learning are heightened when individuals are in caring relationships with others who appreciate their unique talents.

11. Although the basic principles of learning, motivation, and instruction apply to all learners, there are individual differences among students in their learning strategies, learning rates, and unique capabilities in particular areas.

12. All individuals interpret life's experiences according to their unique beliefs and thoughts.

Note. Adapted from "Learner-Centered Psychological Principles: Guidelines for School Redesign and Reform," 1993, American Psychological Association.

which have been substantiated by contemporary research on students' learning and motivation. In this section, we briefly marshal arguments against the "traditional approaches" to curriculum, instruction, and assessment. Our aim, however, is not to lay blame on those who came before us. Instead, our purpose is to discuss some of the ways in which, in our view, these approaches work against students' and teachers' personal development.

Traditional Curriculum and Instruction

Throughout the 20th century, curricula in K–12 have become more specialized and more fractionated. One reason is that knowledge about each subject domain has increased tremendously, so there is more information to teach students about English, social studies, algebra, and so forth. Even in elementary grades, there has been greater attention to teaching specific writing skills, number knowledge, and science concepts at younger ages. A second reason is that with more information to teach, there is competition for students' time, so that separate periods of time have been established for different subjects at different grade levels. American students spend most of their time in K–3 involved in language arts activities, followed by mathematics, with anything else coming in a distant third place.

> Psychological theories and research provide principles of development, teaching, motivation, and learning that can guide educational reforms.

What has led to this fractionated curriculum? There are many forces, including professional teaching organizations for separate curricular areas, separate textbooks and materials, and separate assessments and standards. By second or third grade, most students are evaluated in reading and math with standardized tests that are used to measure the success of the students and schools alike. Yes, tests drive the curriculum and the amount of time that teachers devote to specific skills and concepts, because if the information is not going to be tested, most teachers say they do not have the time to teach it. Is it any wonder that students develop the same attitudes and ask the most frequently heard question in college classrooms, "Is this going to be on the test?"

We think that traditional curricula inhibit students' self-regulated learning by compartmentalizing teaching and learning according to brief exercises, discrete workbooks, and distinct time blocks for each subject area. Tests proscribed by curricular materials often determine what is important to learn, with students lacking any choice or control. Curricula are designed to provide the same knowledge to all students, with little attention to differences in interests or backgrounds. Thus, some students become frustrated with the tedious pace of the material, whereas others become frustrated by the difficulty of the same information (Rohrkemper & Corno, 1988). Teachers resort to group lessons, lectures, and repeated testing to assure that students memorize the information at least once. Teaching is reduced to telling, and learning is reduced to passing a test. Curricula remain disjointed for many students who never have opportunities to integrate and apply their knowledge. Instruction remains monotonous for both teachers and students. If there was any self-regulated learning among students in early grades, several years of listening to directions, filling out dittoed worksheets, and studying for tests usually suppresses independence and intrinsic motivation by high school.

> Traditional curricula inhibit students' self-regulated learning by compartmentalizing teaching and learning.

Traditional Assessment

Every teacher knows that some students have extraordinary difficulty taking academic tests. Some students are so anxious about tests that they become physically ill. Others fidget, ask to use the bathroom, talk to other children, or daydream. Some become confused by the test and give up. They may mark answers haphazardly, make up their own game on the answer sheet, cheat, or simply leave answers blank. Some students do not monitor their time and pace; most do not check their answers. Recently, Michigan teachers gave fourth graders a statewide reading achievement test that included 17 pages of text and questions on the Roman Empire. It was an untimed test, and teachers reported that some students broke down in exasperation, some marked answers without looking back in the passage, and others spent several hours trying to figure out the answers. Was this a valid test of reading comprehension?

We need to examine the impact of traditional testing practices on students. Do traditional achievement tests provide accurate measures of children's academic knowledge and learning skills? How does testing affect students' learning and motivation? Rarely are these kinds of questions raised on behalf of the students because policymakers usually focus on the political and psychometric aspects of testing. First, let us consider the politics of testing. Political issues surrounding testing boil down to accountability to authority (Resnick & Resnick, 1990). Students should be accountable to teachers, teachers should be accountable to principals, principals should be accountable to school district administrators who are in turn accountable to school boards, and so on through state and federal levels. The hierarchy of accountability is imposed externally on teachers and students who are often disenfranchised from all decision making. Teachers do not have opportunities to choose the tests or comment on whether they measure the curriculum provided in the classroom. Yet they must provide summative information on the basis of minimal data about students' performance and are held accountable for the results.

Policymakers at every level compare performance among teachers, school districts, and states with the explicit goal of identifying those who score more poorly than others. Accountability in this scenario is reduced to competition among educators on the basis of comparisons of test scores. The consequences of test scores are quite variable. Most newspapers publish test scores for each school and district, many districts allocate

> The cumulative effects of learning in order to pass tests discourages intrinsic motivation as students progress through school.

resources and money to schools on the basis of test scores, and some districts determine tenure and merit pay decisions with test scores. Teachers as well as students are demeaned by these practices.

The politics of testing in this model doom half of all students and teachers to failure because, in a fair test, half will score below average. Even criterion-referenced tests produce a large number of participants who score below others because the cutoff scores are established by political motives to show the relatively good or poor performance of the test takers. The focus on failure and extrinsic motivation sends the wrong message to students and parents. Many educators and psychologists believe that competition and comparison should not be the basis for accountability because it puts all of the emphasis on high test scores instead of self-motivated learning for intrinsic interests and improvement.

Another problem with traditional politics of accountability is that the participants have no voice in the process. If teachers or students feel the tests are unfair or inappropriate, they will not be committed to doing their best. If the participants do not understand the test or disagree with the uses and interpretations of the results, they are unlikely to perceive the tests as useful or valid (Valencia & Pearson, 1987). The traditional politics of accountability are totalitarian, not democratic, and they produce feelings of estrangement, distrust, and skepticism rather than ownership, responsibility, and commitment.

> Traditional politics of accountability produce feelings of estrangement, distrust, and skepticism rather than ownership, responsibility, and commitment.

These consequences were not intended by the test designers and are not disruptive to the lives and educational success of many students, but it is alarming that the negative consequences are unacknowledged and uncorrected for the many students who suffer labels, tracking, anxiety, and lost opportunities because of standardized testing (see Paris, 1994).

Let us consider the psychometric approaches to traditional achievement testing. In addition to political authorities, the chief decision makers regarding educational assessment are testing specialists who often evaluate the effectiveness of tests in terms of validity and reliability. The acknowledged variability among teachers in how they prepare students for tests and the variability among students in their motivation for the tests are regarded as "noise" or extraneous variance. They are not seen as important individual differences, although Haladyna, Nolen, and Haas (1991) have recently referred to variable test preparation activities as "test pollution" to indicate these sources of contamination. The primary purpose of most achievement tests is to rank order or sort students from worst to best according to scores. Students' scores can be aggregated to provide summary information about classrooms, schools, and districts, which can also be ranked. Many critics argue that the tests are not diagnostic; they do not help teachers because these tests are often not aligned with their curricula. Test results, which may arrive months later, are often incomprehensible because few teachers or parents understand the standard deviations, standardized scores, and statistical interpretations of the scores. The scores are rarely used to inform instructional decision making. When testing is conducted at the end of the year, the scores often do not even arrive in the schools before students leave for the summer, so that the reports are useless for teachers and students. Other critics argue that the tests drive instruction, they narrow the curriculum, they devalue teachers' judgments, and they establish inappropriate goals of education (see Madaus & Tan, 1993).

Traditional achievement tests become "high-stakes" tests for the participants, but the political and psychometric emphases in testing ignore the impact on teachers and students. That is why we have argued that the students' psychological perspectives are fundamental to the effectiveness and validity of any educational assessment (Paris, Lawton, & Turner, 1992). It is surprising, and maybe unethical, that students' perceptions of testing, which are so important for performance and so obvious to teachers, are neglected by policymakers and testing specialists. We surveyed almost 2,000 students from grades 2 through 11 in four states to find out what they think of standardized tests (Paris, Lawton, Turner, & Roth, 1991). The results can be summarized in three developmental trends. First, there was a growing suspicion about the validity and usefulness of the tests. Elementary students generally thought that standardized achievement tests measured how smart they were, and they believed that the tests were useful to parents and teachers. Older students were more cynical about the purposes, uses, and accuracy of tests. The second trend was decreasing motivation and effort with increasing age. Young students tried to do their best, but older students admitted that they often did not care and did not try to do well. Part of their decreased effort may be due to their worries that other students would find out their test scores; they deliberately did not try their best so that the score would not reflect their performance accurately. This kind of self-protection of competence through diminished effort is a common strategy in schools where competition and public comparison of academic ability are prevalent. The third trend was the surprising increase with age in counterproductive test-taking strategies. Older students reported that they did not have good test-taking strategies, that they often guessed or filled in bubbles without thinking, and that they did not bother to check their answers.

> Traditional achievement testing, even when done with the best of intentions, may undermine self-regulated learning.

These three developmental trends are of course interrelated and not evident for all students. We divided students into high and low achievers and discovered that the negative attitudes and behaviors were much more frequent among low-achieving students. It seems reasonable that students who have histories of trying hard and scoring poorly on these tests would become embittered and cynical and adopt counterproductive strategies such as random guessing. The irony is that these invalid and low test scores become self-fulfilling prophecies for these students. The tests are least accurate, least helpful, and most anxiety-producing for the most needy students, low achievers.

Achievement testing, even when done with the best of intentions, may unwittingly counteract each characteristic of self-regulated learning that we identified. We will consider each of the seven characteristics in turn:

☐ Neither teachers nor students have many choices about the tests they take, when they take them, or how the results are used.

☐ Standardized testing, grading on the curve, and normative comparisons of performance inhibit risk taking and optimism because half of the population will always score below the average.

☐ Most traditional achievement tests do not allow students to control the pace of administration and do not depend on the self-controlled learning strategies that they use on a daily basis to seek and clarify information.

☐ Testing is solitary and competitive, which prohibits help seeking and collaborative learning and contradicts many instructional practices.

☐ Traditional achievement tests inhibit appropriate text comprehension because (a) the passages are often brief, contrived, and decontextualized; (b) the multiple-choice format restricts opportunities to express constructed meaning adequately; and (c) the test format fosters strategies of searching for answers in text rather than reading the text for meaning.

☐ The consequences of standardized testing may be devastating for many students because the costs of increased anxiety and self-doubt outweigh any individual diagnostic help provided by the test results.

☐ Traditional tests do not assess students' awareness of their own learning processes and do not provide opportunities for students to use the metacognitive strategies that teachers emphasize on a daily basis.

For all of these reasons, traditional achievement testing decouples self-regulated learning from assessments and destabilizes students' feelings of self-efficacy, self-determination, and personal responsibility. Regardless of the psychometric properties of the tests, the ways they are used can suppress motivation and learning in schools. The negative consequences of standardized testing have been ignored because of public and political pressures for educational accountability and comparative, quantifiable measures of students' achievement. Greater accountability, however, has stimulated searches for "new and better" tests, which, unfortunately, has spawned a range of new commercial, statewide, and national tests. Although some of these new approaches are more authentic assessments of students' learning, the renewed emphasis on assessment has resulted in more testing, with more dire consequences (e.g., diploma certification) imposed on schools with little attention given to the impact of more frequent testing on students' learning and motivation.

It is time for a more balanced view of assessment policies in schools, in which the liabilities and benefits of assessment are discussed openly. The impact of assessment on the quality of teaching and learning must be evaluated. The attitudes of teachers and students must be surveyed so that we are sure that the next generation of assessments elicits their genuine endorsement. This means that teachers and students alike should perceive the assessments as valid, informative, and useful. We recognize that the brief presentation in this chapter is not balanced. The strengths of standardized achievement testing, such as efficiency, economy, and comparisons on the same quantitative scales, are already well known. There are many advocates for the use of such tests, and a large number of educators believe that those traditional tests can be revised to be satisfactory. There are also other educators who believe strongly that entirely new forms of assessment are required in schools (Wolf, Bixby, Glenn, & Gardner, 1991) in order to promote thoughtfulness. All we have at this time, however, are promises that portfolios and performance assessments can provide more equitable, more authentic, and less corruptible forms of assessment. There is a renewed energy in the debates about test validity and the consequences of assessment for students that will, in the long run, improve educational assessment. We believe that parents, school boards, and policymakers need to reconsider the impact of assessment practices on students so that both ongoing and focused assessments attenuate the negative consequences and enhance the positive aspects of ownership and self-efficacy that fuel self-regulated learning. In the next chapter, we will turn to learner-centered principles of assessment that map new directions for classroom assessment that can serve students and teachers effectively.

1 **Reflecting:** Think about the many ways that you assess students' learning in your classroom, so that you can fill in the columns below. What are the traditional methods of assessment that you use? Which ones do you like? Which ones would you omit or revise if you could?

My traditional assessments	What I like best	What I would change

2 **Responding:** We identified seven characteristics of self-regulated learning. For each of the characteristics, identify one or two activities in your classroom that provide opportunities for students to apply or use the characteristic.

Characteristics of self-regulated learning	Student opportunities in my classroom
Allowing personal choices	
Adjusting the challenge	
Taking control of learning	
Collaboration with others	
Constructing meaning while reading and writing	
Consequences that enhance self-efficacy	
Metacognitive strategies for learning	

3 **Sharing:** Ask your students to make a list on a sheet of paper titled "What Counts in My Classroom." Do not put names on the papers; just the grade level. Have other teachers do the same thing in their classes, and then exchange papers between classes so that each class can discuss what counts in other classrooms. This will be illuminating (and humorous perhaps) for both teachers and students.

4 **Reviewing:** Self-evaluation is a fundamental first step for change. However, we do not need to have students criticize themselves or each other; nor do we need to require that they "grade" their own performance in order to encourage self-evaluation. Instead, they should reflect on their strengths and weaknesses by examining the quality of their work, their habits, and their motivation in order to make plans for future improvement. How often do teachers allow opportunities for students to become aware of their own thinking and learning processes and to take responsibility for their own learning? How much time is allowed for reflection and self-assessment, and how many opportunities are provided for students to be engaged actively in reviewing and discussing their own progress? Teachers can benefit from the same opportunities because the same principles that support self-regulated learning in students apply to teachers. Teachers, like students, are intrinsically motivated when they have choices, challenges, control, and collaboration. Teachers want to construct their own meaningful classroom structures and climates, not follow prescriptions mandated by someone else. Then they can also invest effort and feel proud of their accomplishments so that the consequences of their success are recognized by others and sustain their efforts to teach with enthusiasm and creativity. Reflecting, responding, and sharing ideas is crucial for initiating new educational practices for all the participants in education—students, teachers, parents, and administrators.

SUGGESTED READINGS

Perkins, D. (1992). *Smart schools: From training memories to educating minds*. New York: Macmillan.

Raffini, J. P. (1993).*Winners without losers*. Needham Heights, MA: Allyn & Bacon.

Report of the National Commission on Testing and Public Policy. *From gatekeeper to gateway: Transforming testing in America*. Chestnut Hill, MA: National Commission on Testing and Public Policy, Boston College.

goal two

Understanding Learner-Centered

Principles of Assessment

"**Keeping track is a matter of reflective review and summarizing, in which there is both discrimination and record of the significant features of a developing experience .... It is the heart of intellectual organization and of the disciplined mind.**" John Dewey

The pattern of growing disillusionment, decreased motivation, and detachment from a commitment to academic learning because of the primacy of accountability through standardized testing threatens children's orientations to learning and education. New forms of assessment must be created that are sensitive to students' backgrounds, motivation, affect, and attitudes so that they are positively motivated to do their best. New forms of assessment must establish intrinsic goals of mastery, improvement, and success rather than extrinsic comparative goals based on test scores. New forms of assessment should involve students so that they respect the test purposes, content, and format. Assessment should elicit productive strategies and positive motivation so that students can maximize their performance. These positive features of assessment might be attained through performance testing or portfolios of work samples where assessment is linked to the classroom curriculum and is part of an ongoing process in which students monitor their personal progress.

Students may learn to assess and regulate their own performance when they have the responsibility and motivation to improve their own learning and when all students understand that they can progress and succeed in the classroom (Corno, 1992). Students' perspectives on learning and assessment can have long-lasting consequences for education, and it is imperative that policymakers who are revising assessment practices consider the psychological impact on students as well as the political and psychometric features of assessment. For assessment practices to support the development of self-regulated learning, educators need to become aware of learner-centered principles of assessment. We offer the following list of principles as a guideline for assessment reforms that support students' learning.

These twelve principles are meaningful corollaries to the APA Presidential Task Force's Learner-Centered Psychological Principles and can be applied directly to assessment situations and tasks. There are numerous classroom activities that go along with these principles. In fact, many organizations, such as the National Council for Teachers of Mathematics and the International Reading Association, have proposed assessment frameworks that are compatible with these principles. Our focus in the remaining sections of this book is on classroom assessments that teachers can use to promote deeper insights into students' learning—insights from teachers, parents, and students themselves.

> New forms of assessment must be created that are sensitive to students' backgrounds, knowledge, and attitudes so that students are motivated to do their best.

ASSESSMENTS THAT PROMOTE REFLECTION

In the traditional classroom, student evaluation is typically regarded as the last feature of an instructional plan and is usually conducted by the teacher. Occasionally, students are superficially involved in evaluation when they are given tasks such as correcting each others' spelling or math tests, usually based on an answer key devised by the teacher. However, their insights about how to measure learning are not stimulated, and their opinions are seldom sought. It is the rare classroom in which students regularly collaborate with the teacher, analyze the strengths and weaknesses of their work, assess their attitudes toward their learning, set goals, and identify ways to monitor their progress toward those goals. This is self-appraisal, in which students learn to assess their own work by deciding what is right or wrong, when the task goal is met, and what standards

> It is imperative that policymakers who are revising assessment practices consider the psychological impact on students as well as the political and psychometric features of assessment.

LEARNER-CENTERED PRINCIPLES OF ASSESSMENT

1. The fundamental purpose of any educational assessment of students should be to promote meaningful learning.

2. Assessment should elicit students' genuine effort, motivation, and commitment to the assessment activity and situation.

3. Assessment should provide credibility and legitimacy to a broad range of talents and accomplishments of students across the curriculum.

4. Assessment should occur continuously in classrooms in order to provide longitudinal evidence of individual progress.

5. The strategies, skills, and knowledge required to excel in academic assessments should be the same as those required to master the curriculum on a daily basis.

6. Assessments should be based on authentic and meaningful tasks that are consistent with the regular curriculum and instruction provided in the classroom.

7. Assessments should be fair and equitable to all students regardless of prior achievement, gender, race, language, or cultural background.

8. Assessments should measure students' motivation, attitudes, and affective reactions about the curriculum as well as their cognitive skills, strategies, and knowledge.

9. Assessments should include exhibits, portfolios, and performances to demonstrate a wide range of behavior and accomplishments.

10. The design of standards of excellence and assessment systems should be negotiated by the participants—including parents, teachers, administrators, and students—in districts and states to ensure consensus, commitment, and ownership among the primary stakeholders.

11. The results of assessment should provide clear, comprehensible, and immediate feedback to the participants.

12. All assessments should provide for periodic review and revision among the participants and consumers of assessment information.

are acceptable. It is a completely different level of assessment than merely checking students' work for errors.

Another way to highlight our emphasis on self-assessment is to contrast two types of assessment activities found in most classrooms. One type, the traditional test, is a *focused assessment* because it is designed to measure a specific skill or achievement. Focused assessments include weekly spelling tests, end-of-unit tests, completion of worksheets or fill-in-the-blank forms, and conventional standardized tests. Most of these take a brief amount of time, occur at the end of instruction, and result in a score that is reported. In contrast, *ongoing assessments* are usually part of the regular curriculum and are given several times—often before, during, or after instruction—to measure cognitive and motivational processes as well as products of learning. Focused assessments usually serve summative functions for accountability of group performance, whereas ongoing assessments usually serve formative or diagnostic functions for individuals. Both types are valuable but serve different needs, purposes, and audiences.

Our emphasis is on ongoing assessments because they promote students' analysis and direction of their own learning. When students begin to internalize the roles and knowledge of teachers, they provide their own self-assessments. When teachers value student self-assessment, the focus of evaluation moves from something that is done at the end of a project to something that occurs throughout the learning process. In contrast with traditional testing, we advocate using assessment procedures that are interwoven with learning so that opportunities for teaching and learning are coincident with opportunities for assessment. This is more like coaching in athletics and music, where assessment and instruction are symbiotic and complementary.

We can distinguish at least four characteristics of these types of ongoing assessments that promote self-regulated learning. First, the activities are meaningful to students. They are authentic learning activities that provoke students' curiosity and imagination and sustain attention because they are relevant to personal goals of

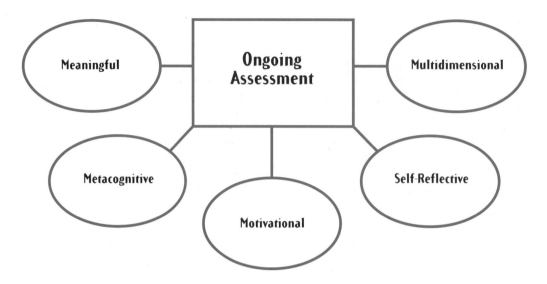

Figure 3: *Characteristics of assessments that promote self-regulation.*

the students. Second, students' reflections are metacognitive and perhaps metamotivational because they are engaged in appraising their own ways of knowing, that is, their cognitive processes and motivational dispositions. We encourage students to reflect on the products and content of their learning, as well as the strategies and processes that they use to acquire knowledge. Third, students are stimulated to reflect on their growth when they assess progress over time. Thus, the tasks are inherently developmental because they encourage students to evaluate themselves over time. Fourth, assessments that promote reflection are multidimensional and lead to variable judgments. For example, students might regard their progress in writing as superior but their progress in arithmetic as less than adequate, or they may regard their motivation as low for reading some kinds of books, compared with other topics or other purposes. Indeed, one of the functions of reflective assessments is to stimulate students to notice their strengths and weaknesses across many areas of academic learning.

STUDENTS' SELF-ASSESSMENT

When students take charge of their own learning, they reflect on their accomplishments, evaluate their work, plan revisions, set goals, and develop positive self-perceptions of their competence. For some, these characteristics are embedded in self-regulated learning, but for others, self-assessment is a topic that deserves attention in its own right. In many other countries, assessment has focused less on accountability and more explicitly on the value of self-assessment for promoting students' active engagement in learning. For example, Towler and Broadfoot (1992) argued that self-assessment should be a fundamental goal of primary schools in England. They wrote, "Reflection and evaluation can encourage understanding of what is expected, improve motivation, lead to pride in positive achievement and offer a realistic appraisal of weaknesses" (p. 138).

Towler and Broadfoot offered four reasons to shift attention from external testing to self-assessment that are relevant to American schools. One reason is that the current reforms of assessment in the United Kingdom emphasize the Records of Achievement in secondary schools, records that depend heavily on students' self-review. Although most American schools do not require self-review or evaluation of progress as part of achievement testing, proficiency testing and portfolios have already been mandated by law for high school graduation in Michigan. A second reason to focus on students' self-assessment, according to Towler and Broadfoot, is that many suggestions for assessment reform are impractical and time-consuming; teachers simply do not have adequate time to collect observational and anecdotal records every day on every student. Third, they argue that self-assessment is compatible with the child-centered principles of primary school education; it is aligned with the curriculum and instruction better than other forms of testing. Fourth, and perhaps most compelling to us, is that self-assessment promotes self-regulated learning. Towler and Broadfoot wrote, "Exercising initiative and responsibility, having a positive influential stake in decisions should lead to increased self-awareness and independence" (p. 138).

Self-assessment deserves special attention from teachers because many students, particularly young children, may need help learning how to assess their academic skills and performance appropriately. Some help is required to focus on relevant sources of feedback and criteria for performance (Stipek & MacIver, 1989). Young children need to know that teachers' approval is not the only form of evaluation and that there are task-specific criteria for performance. This information is necessary so that children do not mistake evaluations of their behavior (e.g., working quietly) as evaluations of their learning. Children may also need help learning to maintain records and provide summaries of their work. Towler and Broadfoot (1992) summarized four phases of self-assessment that are fundamental in their approach to assessment:

> Reflection and evaluation can encourage understanding of what is expected, improve motivation, lead to pride in positive achievement and offer a realistic appraisal of weaknesses.

1. The knowledge phase. Students recall previous experiences, review their work, and provide concrete records.

2. The analysis/understanding phase. Students seek to understand why things happened and to make attributions for their performance.

3. The evaluation phase. Students make judgments about the quality of their work and construct plausible explanations for their evaluations.

4. The synthesis phase. Students organize their new knowledge with past experience, fit their evaluations into a larger context, and set future objectives.

Towler and Broadfoot (1992) suggested that self-assessment is appropriate for 4- to 7-year-olds in primary schools. Although some may think that is too young, skills acquired in these four phases are within the capabilities of children in elementary school. Certainly, 7-year-olds can use them to assess their own reading and writing. Each phase can be expected to improve with age and practice—which is exactly why some educators advocate beginning the processes of self-assessment early. The difficulty that 6- to 8-year-olds may have with penmanship, spelling, and articulating their reflections should not deter the use of self-assessment, because there are many developmentally appropriate activities that teachers can use. We have seen many teachers engage their 5- to 8-year-old students in critical analyses of their own work during oral conferences and reviews of their work samples. These establish a pattern of self-assessment that can become proficient with practice.

Self-assessment is not just relevant for young children; it is important for self-regulated learning at all ages. In an analysis of literacy practices in New Zealand and Australia, van Kraayenoord (1993) pointed out that self-assessment promotes students' senses of ownership and responsibility, two critical aspects of literacy development that must be nurtured throughout students' schooling. She suggested that teachers in all grades can foster self-assessment by encouraging students to

◻ examine artifacts that they create,

◻ review progress through record keeping,

◻ document their interests, choices, and preferences,

◻ confer with teachers,

◻ write collaboratively, and

◻ share personal responses.

Teachers in New Zealand and Australia routinely use a wide variety of activities for these purposes, such as reading logs, journals, goal statements, and conferences. These approaches are supported by state and federal programs of professional development for teachers, and the emphasis on self-assessment is consistent with new standards in literacy, language arts, and mathematics throughout Australia and New Zealand. Performance-based assessment has been used for many years in these countries, rather than standardized testing, which has led to shared understanding among teachers and parents about the value of self-assessment. Such consensus building about the value of self-assessment is just beginning in many American schools.

There are additional arguments for teachers to emphasize self-assessment in their classrooms. It reduces the workload of teachers because students take the responsibility for collecting and monitoring their records. Students' reactions and evaluations may improve the curriculum by pointing out approaches that do not work and topics that deaden student interest. Self-assessment means that students can share their school performance more intelligibly with their parents. However, the most important reason may be that self-assessment contributes to authentic, learner-centered assessment practices that promote learning, not just accountability. Towler and Broadfoot (1992) conclude,

> Self-assessment is a vital aspect of primary education in England, Australia, and New Zealand.

> The efforts of individual teachers and schools are already beginning to indicate that the principle of collaboration in assessment is both valid and realistic in the context of contemporary schooling. The pursuit of such practices further demonstrates the determination of the professionals in education to resist politically-inspired attempts to return to traditional methods of assessment by strengthening and extending the examination system. For the professionals, the priority must remain the development of practices which increase pupils' confidence, which motivate them to learn more and which equip them with the understanding to do this. (p. 151)

We began this book by highlighting specific features of Joanie's third grade classroom in order to provide a realistic and concrete description of authentic activities that teachers can use to stimulate reflections about students' learning. They are "high stakes" activities because they have enduring consequences for students' lifelong learning. We have traced the motivational, metacognitive, and strategic aspects of learner-centered assessment to reveal the principles and dynamics of self-assessment. Now we will return to practical concerns of the classroom and describe how teachers can create environments in which self-assessment and reflection are daily, functional activities. In the following sections we will describe activities used by teachers to promote reflection among students, parents, and teachers. The descriptions are based on actual materials created by teachers, to illustrate the activities and to exhibit typical student responses.

1 **Reflecting:** Consider the motivational consequences of different kinds of assessments that students receive in school as you examine the matrix below and complete the self-assessment column. Reflect on the "Sharing Activity" at the end of Goal 1, in which students responded to the question, "What counts in my classroom?" Do they have a focus on external standards provided by assessments, or do they focus on their personal standards reflected in their own work? Why do they have this focus and how does it affect their motivation?

Forms of Assessment

Issues	Report cards	Test scores	Self-assessment
What are the outcomes?	Grades	Numbers	
Who is being compared?	Class	Large populations	
Who is in control?	Teacher	Policymakers	
What is the student's role?	Passive	Passive	

2 **Responding:** Think about the opportunities in your class for students to evaluate their own performance and progress. Identify the activities and students' reactions to them in the columns below.

Self-assessment activities	Students' reactions

3

Sharing: Review the 12 learner-centered principles for assessment with other teachers and discuss how these might be adopted as School Principles or outcomes in your own district. Present the principles in this book along with your own principles to your local Parent–Teacher Association or School Improvement Team for their discussion.

4

Reviewing: As you review what students say counts in your school, consider how your assessment practices foster those views. Think about the costs and benefits of students' orientations to external and internal standards and how students' views become cumulative as they progress through school. We have listed the principles of learning and assessment that place primary emphasis on the student's involvement, motivation, and attitudes so that assessment activities can support rather than inhibit autonomous learning. We hope that these principles stimulate discussions among teachers and community groups about the roles of students in assessment activities. One of our goals in this book is to broaden the traditional use of assessment beyond educational accountability to promote students' motivation and self-regulated learning.

SUGGESTED READINGS

Darling-Hammond, L. (1991). The implications of testing policy for quality and equity. *Phi Delta Kappan, 73,* 220–225.

Hymes, D. L., Chafin, A. E., & Gonder, P. (1991). *The changing face of testing and assessment.* Arlington, VA: American Association of School Administrators.

Johnston, P. H. (1992). *Constructive evaluation of literate activity.* New York: Longman.

Wolf, D., Bixby, J., Glenn, J., & Gardner, H. (1991). To use their minds well: Investigating new forms of student assessment. In G. Grant (Ed.), *Review of research in education* (Vol. 17, pp. 31–74). New York: American Educational Research Association.

goal three

Promoting Students' Reflections
Through Classroom Activities

"The whole art of teaching is only the art of awakening the natural curiosity of young minds for the purpose of satisfying it afterwards." Anatole France

In this section we will describe four general types of classroom activities that teachers can use to promote students' reflections. These activities include (a) portfolios, (b) surveys and inventories, (c) journals and letters, and (d) various kinds of conferences. Each activity is used by teachers to engage students in self-evaluations of their work and abilities.

We provide brief descriptions of these tools and their uses in the classroom and illustrate them with concrete examples from children. Our purpose is to persuade teachers that these activities can easily be incorporated in their daily instruction and that students and teachers alike gain a considerable amount of shared insight into students' learning through the interactions initiated and sustained with these activities.

USING PORTFOLIOS TO ENHANCE SELF-ASSESSMENT

During the last 5 years, educators around the world have enthusiastically embraced the use of portfolios for student assessment (Glazer & Brown, 1993; Graves & Sunstein, 1992; Herman, Aschbacher, & Winters, 1992; Tierney, Carter, & Desai, 1991; van Kraayenoord & Paris, 1992; Weeks & Leaker, 1991). Portfolios have been used by students at all grade levels from kindergarten through university and in core academic subjects as well as performing arts and vocational skills. Some of the enthusiasm for portfolios is due to their broad and adaptable applications to diverse subjects; however, some is due to teachers taking control of their own assessments and seeing the benefits directly in their students. Portfolios have been endorsed because they offer viable alternatives, or at least meaningful supplements, to traditional testing, and because portfolios can foster self-regulated learning in ways that testing cannot.

> Portfolios can provide exhibits of students' accomplishments from kindergarten to college across diverse subjects.

We (the coauthors) began our collaboration several years ago when we designed a portfolio system for teachers in a suburban Detroit school district. Because many of our examples are drawn from teachers in that district, it is worthwhile to provide a synopsis of our Portfolio Project. Basically, we invited K–6 teachers to volunteer to experiment with portfolios in their classrooms. We provided them materials and workshops to support their use of portfolios. We emphasized the need to proceed slowly, in small steps, with lots of collaboration and feedback. Now in its second year, the pilot project has had nearly 90% of the teachers in the district volunteer to participate. The physical system was a portable file bin in each classroom that contained hanging folders for each student's work. The conceptual system was essentially a "menu of options" of things that teachers might include in the portfolios.

The initial question faced by teachers who want to use portfolios is, "What should I collect?" Too many teachers who begin portfolios without a clear view of their purpose collect everything that students produce and hope that they can sort out what is important later. Some never do. That is why we advocate that teachers, individually or collectively, identify the dimensions of learning that they value enough to assess and report. One system for identifying fundamental dimensions of literacy is described by Paris, Calfee, et al. (1992). The seven dimensions of literacy development that seem important for students in all elementary schools include

☐ engagement with text through reading,

☐ engagement with text through writing,

☐ knowledge about literacy,

☐ orientation to literacy,

☐ ownership of literacy,

☐ collaboration, and

☐ connectedness of the curriculum.

Each of these dimensions can be elaborated in order to provide more specific indicators of progress that can be measured. However, we recognize that most teachers do not have the time or opportunity to create such a list of dimensions on their own, and so they use their intuitions to guide the collection of portfolio materials. When we created our portfolio project, we recognized that these dimensions are similar to many report card categories of language arts, so we turned to the district's report card as a guide for what to collect in portfolios. This provided a familiar scheme for teachers in the district and turned out to be a critical linchpin.

One key to the success of the Walled Lake Portfolio Project was the principled and selective collection of work from students. Another key was fitting the portfolios into existing assessment procedures in the district. Both objectives were met by one design feature: We used report cards to help define the kinds of evidence that should be collected in the portfolios. Because we focused on language arts, we used the categories of literacy behaviors and skills on the report cards to inform teachers about the kinds of work to collect: that is, work that would support judgments about behaviors such as "reads independently, recognizes literary elements, writes for a variety of purposes, and revises content." This procedure can readily be extended to other subject areas so that portfolios provide support for judgments that teachers make across the curriculum.

Using the report card categories had many beneficial spin-offs. One was that teachers could easily communicate the importance of the portfolios to parents and children. Second, teachers saw the connections between the portfolios, daily classroom work, and periodic assessment reports. Third, teachers and administrators created a set of literacy standards and performance indicators based on the report card categories and the kinds of authentic evidence that teachers collect. Finally, we should also note that using the report cards as a starting point for identifying valued outcomes and authentic classroom evidence often leads teachers and administrators to reexamine and revise their report cards. This is a vivid illustration of the power of reflection and the need to realign assessment evidence and reports with curricula periodically throughout a district.

Although we initially used report cards, we added several layers of additional information to the categories to help teachers know what to collect. We created a matrix of the 11 language arts categories crossed with 3 kinds of evidence to illustrate different aspects of students' accomplishments. The 3 kinds of evidence were based on students' Performances, Processes, and Perceptions because we wanted teachers to examine children's strategies and attitudes as well as their actual work. Evidence of Performance included written stories and reports, lists of books children had read, and other finished work samples. Evidence of Processes included rough drafts of children's writing, strategy assessments, and teachers' observations of learning and behavior. Evidence of Perceptions included students' self-reports of attitudes, motivation, and academic progress.

> The portfolios were functional and embedded in other assessment practices of teachers, yet each teacher determined what evidence would be collected in his or her own classroom.

In one workshop early in the school year, teachers worked in grade level groups to fill in the matrix (created by crossing the 3 Ps by the 11 categories) with various assessment activities such as miscue analyses, journals, attitude surveys, and book reports. They shared ideas and created their own individual classroom plans for collecting evidence about each aspect of students' work. These would be the basis for completing student report cards, as well as for conferences with parents. Thus, the portfolios were functional and embedded in other assessment practices of teachers, yet each teacher determined what evidence would be collected in his or her own classroom.

In subsequent workshops, visits, and school-level meetings, teachers were provided with models of activities that other teachers had used. Some of these models were disseminated by the Michigan Department of Education, some were copied from professional journals and books, and some were designed by other teachers around the country. We stored these materials in School Resource Files in each building so that teachers could review and select activities that suited their students. These files were designed to grow over time as teachers added new ideas that they gathered from readings, workshops, and other sources, so that each school staff could develop a sense of ownership for the materials they collected and used.

The transition from knowledge-building to implementation followed the same principles that we encouraged teachers to use with their students: review, reflection, synthesis, selection, and application. The teachers were introduced to the idea of portfolio assessment at faculty meetings by members of the district language arts committees. These committees, along with the elementary principals' instructional council, had been involved in the planning stages of the project since the beginning. By the time the project was suggested at the school level, it had undergone several revisions by teachers and administrators. We feel that the unanimous support this project enjoyed from these groups was an important factor that contributed to its momentum and helped to ensure its success when it reached the implementation phase. We also developed a shared vision for implementation as a 2- to 3-year process and encouraged patience from teachers and administrators. In retrospect, some of the success of the Walled Lake Portfolio Project was due to adherence to the same keys to intrinsic motivation in students; we provided teachers with choices, challenges, control, and collaboration. Later, it was evident from teachers' comments how portfolios changed their beliefs and practices.

Now it is time to turn to descriptions of what teachers did and how they used portfolios and classroom activities to stimulate students' reflections. We will highlight three ways that portfolios can enhance self-assessment: students' creation of portfolios, selection of work, and personal evaluation.

Creating Personal Portfolios

Portfolios offer a concrete way for students to learn to value their own work. When students are responsible for deciding what to include in a portfolio, they are forced to examine their work from new perspectives. For example, in our project, students became aware of the importance of evaluating their Performances, Processes, and Perceptions because these were the frameworks that teachers used. The collaborative portfolio classroom encourages students to use multiple criteria for evaluation, for example, to view their work in terms of effort expended, quality demonstrated, and relative satisfaction with the final product. We do not think the emphasis should only be on including the "best work" in portfolios. Instead, a wide variety of representative work samples will allow students to see their progress from first to final drafts and from journal entries early in the year to late in the year, and to see their positive as well as inappropriate attitudes and strategies.

> When students are responsible for deciding what to include in a portfolio, they are forced to examine their work from new perspectives.

As students consider work samples to include, they should be encouraged to think carefully about the good points of the work and what it conveys about them. They need to consider if it will demonstrate their accomplishments to others and provide a positive indication of their progress. Selecting work is necessarily evaluative, but students need concrete guidelines for analyzing their work. The "Why I Like It Sheet" was designed for this purpose. It provides a structure to help the student examine and articulate the merits of the piece selected for the portfolio. On the sheet, students are encouraged to state what they think is noteworthy about the work they have chosen. For example, it may show unusual effort on the student's part; it may demonstrate a newly mastered skill or process; it may display a point of pride; or it may show improvement in a particular area. We designed the "Why I Like It Sheet" to help students reflect on the reasons for selecting work samples to be included in their portfolios. Figure 4 shows that one child selected a piece because of effort: "I studied 'till my brains couldn't grow any bigger." Figure 5 shows what a fifth-grader included in her portfolio and why one piece is her favorite. It shows clearly that portfolios are unique collections for every child and that children are thoughtful about why they select things for inclusion.

Selecting Work for Classroom Exhibitions and Home Portfolios

In a collaborative portfolio classroom, students have regular opportunities to review their work. As students review their portfolios, they should be encouraged to organize them in a way that makes sense. They may be organized chronologically, by subject area, or in order of preference. As they organize the contents, students should be aware of why each piece has been included in the portfolio, noting what each piece demonstrates about their reading and writing progress. The students may use a table of contents to organize their portfolios or separate folders for different subject areas.

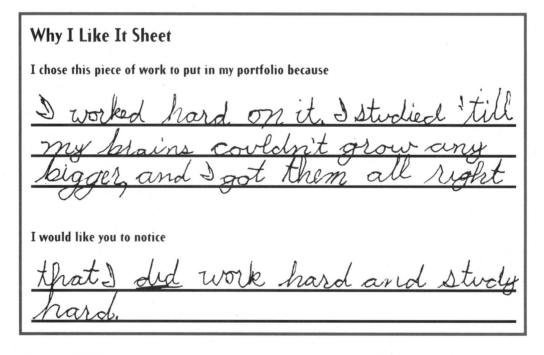

Why I Like It Sheet

I chose this piece of work to put in my portfolio because

I worked hard on it. I studied 'till my brains couldn't grow any bigger, and I got them all right

I would like you to notice

that I did work hard and study hard.

Figure 4: *Children are encouraged to state the reasons for selecting work samples for their portfolios.*

Portfolio Evaluation

Name _Emily_

Date _5-27-93_

A list of all the things in my portfolio:

Fifth Grade Writing Prompt   Spelling Story

Letter to Mrs. H.   Comic strips

Animal Story   Be a Star form

Writing Buddy   Soc. Studies Refletions

Pre Conference   Pond notes

Midterm Reports Reflections

Island of Blue Dolphin

Lansing Reflection

Parent Letter

Open House story

Select your favorite piece from your portfolio and tell me
why it is your favorite!

My Open House Story I think is the best story I've ever written. I made good illustrations and it is funny.

Figure 5: *An example of a fifth-grader's portfolio contents.*

Once included in the portfolio, each entry is viewed in the context of the surrounding pieces, which allows students to see their progress over time, observe trends in performance, and note areas of proficiency. When do these magical reviews happen? Sometimes students peruse their portfolios without prompting, perhaps when they add or examine something. However, teachers can structure periodic opportunities for review. Two successful activities that we have suggested to teachers are the Classroom Portfolio Day and the Home Portfolio. Both set aside time for students to review and reflect on the items in their portfolios.

A Classroom Portfolio Day is an opportunity for all students to review their portfolios, make sure they are complete, and prepare them for someone else to examine. We designed this day as a personal review for students, but some teachers elect to make the exhibits of student work more public. Some teachers choose 4 or 5 students to display their work around the room or building on Portfolio Day. Others may have all students exhibit their work in the classroom. The underlying purpose of the Portfolio Day is to allow students to view each other's work, because it brings pride as well as

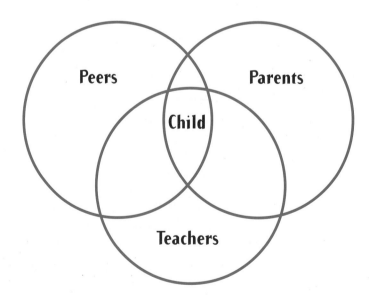

Figure 6: *Audiences for portfolio reviews.*

showing peer achievements, both highly motivating circumstances. Ideally, the Classroom Portfolio Day will occur several days before student–teacher conferences so that the students' reviews help prepare them for their conferences.

We designed Home Portfolios to communicate assessment information between teachers and parents. Teachers and students may decide to cull the portfolio contents at various times during the year, retaining pieces that represent the range of their work as important indicators of progress. Other pieces may be taken home and retained in a Home Portfolio where the child's work may be kept by parents to appreciate throughout the year. Before work is taken home, students should write a letter to parents detailing what is in the folder and what these contents indicate about them so that they reflect on the work and their parents' reactions.

Prior to initiating Classroom Portfolio Days and The Home Portfolio, teachers may write letters of explanation to the parents and distribute them at the beginning of the year. A sample letter is shown below.

Dear Parents,

We are as excited as the students to start the new school year and wanted to take this opportunity to describe our new Portfolio Project to you. Throughout the year, children will collect samples of their work in their own special portfolios in the classroom. We will review these periodically to talk about the progress and accomplishments of each student. Many times during the year your child will bring home things from the portfolio for you to review and save. We hope you will start a "Home Portfolio" to collect this work.

When your child brings home school work, please sit down and go through it together. Ask questions about the portfolios, why it was collected, and what it shows about your child's accomplishments. This conversation will help you understand what your child has been studying and learning at school. More importantly, the Home Portfolio will provide a way for students to share their pride in their work. As always, we welcome your comments and appreciate your support.

Sincerely,

In addition to encouraging students' self-reflection, the Home Portfolio enhances communication between parents and teachers and strengthens parents' appreciation of students' work. For some parents, the Home Portfolio is the most important way that they can learn about the curriculum in school and what teachers ask students to do. It provides a window to the classroom that is crucial for many parents who may feel uninformed or disenfranchised from school. A form like the one shown in Appendix A at the end of the chapter can be used to elicit parents' reactions to students' work, whether or not Home Portfolios are used.

Evaluating and Summarizing Portfolios

After the students have reviewed work collected in their portfolios, they need to evaluate and summarize their reactions. We encouraged teachers to use Portfolio Summary Sheets, which include space for both students' and teachers' comments. Following a review, before a student–teacher conference, students would complete the student portion of the Summary Sheet. The Portfolio Summary Sheet is designed to fulfill two purposes: a) to serve as a framework for students' perceptions of their work, and b) to provide a guide for the portfolio conference between teacher and student. Students respond to questions such as "What are your good learning habits?" "How have you improved your reading and writing so far this year?" and "What do you plan to work on next?" To answer those questions, students must look for improvements in their learning, as shown by work in their portfolios. Then they express those changes in a concise statement on the Summary Sheet as a reflection on their learning across a period of time.

After students have completed their portions of the Summary Sheets, teachers review the portfolios for the same purpose. They complete the teacher section independently, noting student strengths and weaknesses from an instructional perspective. When each portion of the Summary Sheet has been completed, it is brought to the student–teacher conference to serve as a guide for discussion and goal setting. It is important that both teacher and student are prepared for the conference by their initial reviews. The conference proceeds rapidly as teacher and student discuss the work samples and set future goals.

| Reading Packet Evaluation | Name __Rana Y.__ |
| | Date __2-8-94__ |

Student's Evaluation	Teacher's Evaluation
How do you feel about the story you are reading, or have just completed? I feel good about the story becaues it is a funny book.	Overal Grades: Comprehesion ___+___ Skill Pages ___+___ Neatness ___+___
What are some things you feel you have done well in this packet? I wrote in complete sentences	Things I really liked about this reading packet: Excellent skill pages Rana! I enjoyed reading your Diary Entries — I can tell you understood the story
What do you think you still need to work on? Reading faster. Is your reading packet neat? yes Did you use complete sentences? yes	You need to work on: Keep up the great work. Practice reading out loud to someone. You need to read louder in group time. I'm very proud of you ♥

Figure 7: *An example of one student's assessment of her classwork.*

SELF-EVALUATIONS, INVENTORIES, AND SURVEYS

Teachers encourage students to think about their work with many kinds of informal worksheets, inventories, and surveys, sometimes copied from resource materials and sometimes created by teachers on handwritten dittoed sheets. For example, in Joanie Moore's third grade, students evaluate their reading packets periodically by responding to the questions shown in Figure 7. The teacher fills out the other side of the form with her evaluation, shares it with the student, and then slips the form into the student's portfolio.

Similar self-evaluations can be used with daily work whether or not teachers use portfolios. For example, Figure 8 shows a form that students can use to evaluate their own expository writing. They can also record their teachers' suggestions so that the entire record keeping is done by the students. This form is subtle in the way it focuses students' attention on characteristics of expository text structure.

Inventories can be directed at work samples or more general strategies, habits, interests, and attitudes. A fourth-grade teacher encouraged students to think about their reading strategies with the worksheet "Evaluating My Own Reading" shown in Figure 9.

Other teachers use inventories to assess children's attitudes, habits, and interests, as shown in Appendices B and C at the end of the chapter. Even first graders can respond to visual cues such as "happy faces" that signal their reactions. The complexity of the scales and items can be made appropriate to any developmental level. These kinds of self-evaluations can be valuable to teachers early in the year as they become familiar with new students because they allow teachers to identify students' special interests, talents, or problems.

Teachers in grades 6 through 8 use surveys to help students identify their interests and habits, which may be used as the basis for forming groups or selecting projects. Inventories and surveys can also reveal students' favorite books, companions, and games as well as their

Summary of Expository Text

Name Krisi   Date march 3

Components of a Good Summary	Student Self-Assessment	Teacher Assessment
I included a clear main idea statement	✕	+
I included important ideas supporting the main idea.	+	+
My summary shows that I understand the relationships between important concepts	+	✓
I used my own words rather than words copied from the text	+	✓

My teacher's comments on my strengths in writing a summary:

Good beginning — You included the important events in the Lewis and Clark expedition. Very thorough

My teacher's comments on possible improvements:

Make sure your ideas follow a sequence. End your report with a conclusion.

Figure 8: *An example of a student's assessment of an assignment.*

Evaluating My Own Reading   Name _Eric A_

Date _11-22-91_

1. What strategies do you use to figure out words that you don't know?

I take a guess about what it means.

Do you mean you use context clues?

2. Before you begin to read a fiction book, what strategies do you use?

I read the back cover — Good

3. Before you read an informational book, do you use any strategies?

I get out a non-fiction book report form

Do you ever use KWL strategies?

4. Do you ever stop and check for understanding? If you have trouble, what strategies do you use?

I look in my pocket dictionary.   Do you ever re-read?

5. Have you improved your reading over the past few weeks?

Yes because I can read more books per week.

6. What reading goal will you set for next week?

Read five books   Different genre?

Figure 9: *How one teacher promotes a student's self-assessment of reading.*

views of their academic strengths and weaknesses. Other teachers use specific surveys of students' writing and spelling, like the ones shown in Appendices D and E at the end of the chapter, to provoke reflections on students' performance, processes, and perceptions, the three parts of authentic evidence in this particular district. Other teachers use surveys and inventories that are more personal evaluations, such as "How I See Myself As a Reader" in Appendix F at the end of the chapter. This instrument asks children to make judgments about themselves as readers across many different characteristics and is appropriate for children in grades 4 through 8. The intent is to inform students of the variety of characteristics that describe good readers as well as to promote children's reflections on their own particular talents.

One teacher helps students to evaluate their own growing responsibility by checking the kinds of things they do often. She believes that when children attend consciously to these characteristics, they are more likely to follow them. The inventory shown below can be adapted to almost any area of self-evaluation.

Name _____ Date _____

Check Your Responsibilities

How often do you.....	Never	Usually	Always
Listen carefully to other students			
Complete work on time			
Follow directions			
Ask for assistance when needed			
Set a good example for others			
Show courtesy to teachers			
Clean up your desk and locker			

Some teachers have created a simple response format for students to indicate the strength of their agreement with various statements. Students simply draw a line to respond to each item; the longer the line, the stronger the agreement. For example, students might be given a series of statements such as "I like to read," "I know how to skim for information," and "I like to write fiction" and asked to draw lines to indicate whether they agree with each item. It is a method that is easy to use for young children or nonreaders. The items can include self-reports about strategy use as well as attitudes and habits.

We have observed teachers using a wide variety of forms for self-evaluation and inventories before and after assignments to probe children's understanding of their own thinking. We do not advocate compiling these in a set of black-line masters or dittos and used as seat work assignments because then the process of self-assessment may be in danger of being routinized and overused. Teachers need to create their own materials to prompt self-assessment, and use them sparingly and judiciously or else students may offer mechanical responses that they think their teachers want to hear.

> Portfolios should NOT become collections of dittoed worksheets and inventories; teachers need to collect samples of students' work and reflections in many formats.

With this caveat in mind, we offer two more examples. Some teachers in middle grades use self-evaluations of projects several times during the year to provide information about the impact of the assignment, students' efforts, and their reactions to the projects. For example, one teacher used the following questions to encourage reflection on a recently completed group project.

Project Self-Evaluation

What did you like about this project?

What would have made this project better?

What are you most proud of?

How hard did you work on this assignment?

What was difficult about this assignment?

What do you know now that you didn't know before? (Be specific)

What grade do you feel your group earned on this project?

Justify your response.

To encourage a larger perspective, at the end of each term all of the students might fill out a form like the "Semester Reflections" shown in Appendix G at the end of the chapter, which provokes reflections from both students and teachers. It is extremely important to remember that not all of these inventories and self-evaluation techniques are used by any one teacher. In our experience, teachers who provide students with selective and occasional opportunities to reflect on their work as part of their ordinary learning efforts had the most thoughtful responses from their students.

JOURNALS, SELF-PORTRAITS, AND LETTERS

Teachers use journals for many different purposes. Some teachers use them for quick-writes, responding to prompts, creative writing, or collections of free writing. These journals are often kept in spiral-bound notebooks, which can be stored easily and examined later for progress, as the teacher did in Figure 10. Other teachers use journals for separate content areas, so students might have journals for reading, writing, math, social studies, and science that they keep in separate notebooks or locations. Students' responses in these journals are directed to the content of the subject area, such as a response to literature, an analysis of a principle in science, or an explanation of a story problem in math. These journals are analytic because students reflect on the information that they have learned as well as the processes that they may have used. Some teachers use the term "writing to learn" when referring to these kinds of journals. They are effective for assessing students' conceptual understanding, plans, and strategies. Journals provide a concrete record of students' responses, self-evaluations, and key concepts that they learn in an ongoing fashion for distinct subject areas.

Still other teachers use journals as vehicles for conversations with students. Perhaps they are called "dialogue journals" because they record a running dialogue between teachers and students. Teachers in lower elementary grades in particular use dialogue journals to

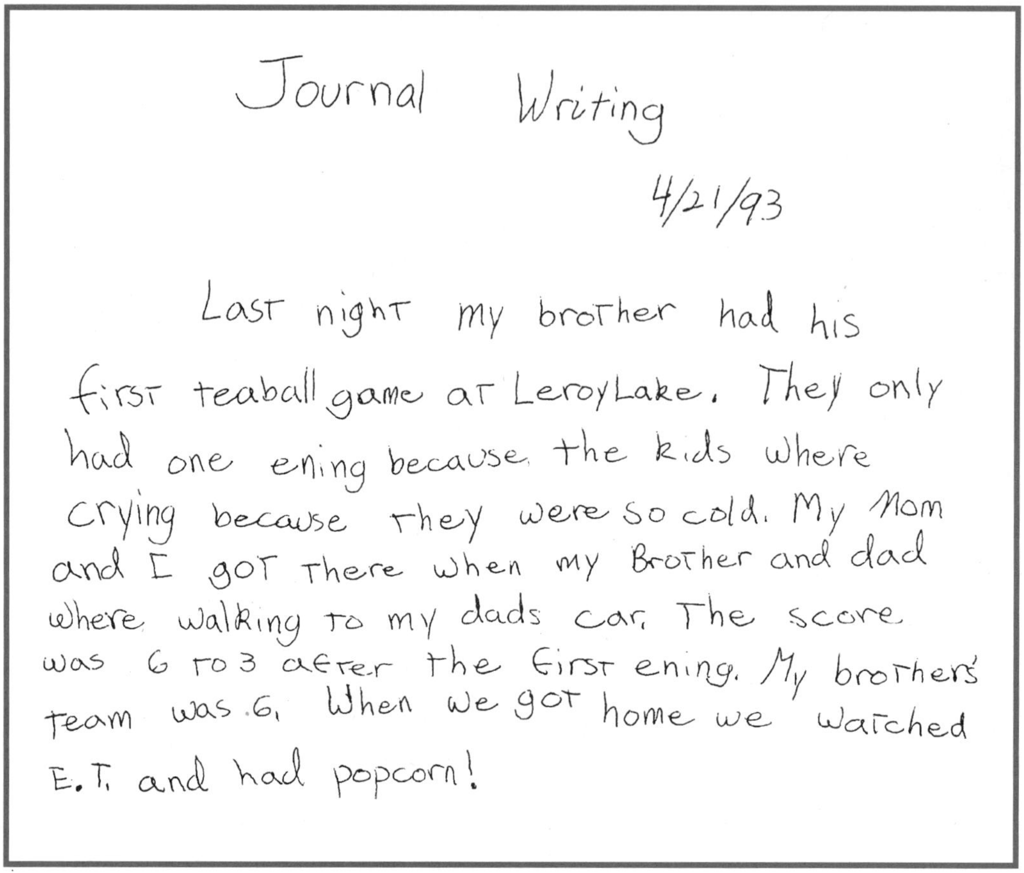

Journal Writing

4/21/93

Last night my brother had his first teaball game at LeroyLake. They only had one ening because the kids where crying because they were so cold. My Mom and I got there when my Brother and dad where walking to my dads car. The score was 6 to 3 after the first ening. My brothers team was 6. When we got home we watched E.T. and had popcorn!

Figure 10: *A first grader's journal entry.*

help children gain fluency in writing, spelling, and self-reflection. Successive journal entries offer vivid illustrations of children's improvements in spelling, handwriting, and expression that parents and children can judge easily over the course of a year. The overriding value of dialogue journals, however, is the content of the conversation. It is fascinating because it is highly personalized and frequently reveals the criteria by which students evaluate their own performance. Young children are often concerned about neatness and the physical appearance of their product, whereas older children are more concerned with the content and ideas expressed in their journals. We have found that students of all ages are surprisingly candid in these conversations with teachers.

The journals establish a personal link to teachers that students take quite seriously. Teachers who use dialogue journals incur an obligation to treat them seriously, to maintain confidentiality, and to reply promptly. That is why teachers often use dialogue journals for a few weeks and then establish "buddy journals" in which students write to classmates or students in a grade above or below their own. This variety relieves pressure from teachers who must respond to all of the journals, and it provides opportunities for peer interactions.

Many teachers are eclectic and combine response journals and dialogue journals in clever ways. Mr. Jackson, a fifth-grade teacher, asked his students to reflect on their learning every Friday afternoon in different journals. One Friday it might be math journals, on the next it might be language arts journals, and on the next Friday it might be science journals, so that each week, students reflected on what they had learned and their reactions to the content and style of instruction. Mr. Jackson replied individually to each student's journal in a creative way. Rather than simply agreeing or commending students' reactions, he probed and challenged them in a constructive manner. Thus, he often asked questions, made connections, and suggested additional searches for information in his conversations with students. This practice had the interesting consequence of eliciting long and thoughtful replies by students, who regarded their conversations as genuine and highly personal.

> Reflections in journals, surveys, and conferences should be elicited occasionally and receive quick feedback so they do not become repetitive or boring.

Journals work as well in college classrooms as they do in elementary classrooms, and we have seen the benefits in our own experiences. For example, we have asked college students to react to reading assignments in an educational psychology class and found amazing richness in the responses of students. At the risk of oversimplifying the diversity of responses, we will focus on the following key characteristics that we have observed in journals to stimulate students' reflections. First, students regard their conversations as personal and candid. They reveal their feelings and reactions willingly and expect the reader to respect the honesty. Second, when teachers minimize the importance of spelling and mechanics in the journal, students provide divergent and creative thoughts. Many times, the journal entries read like a stream of consciousness with quick reactions, incomplete sentences, and ungrammatical constructions, yet provocative ideas. Without the stress of organizing one's thoughts into coherent paragraphs and sentences, students often feel "permission" to be expansive and creative. Third, journals are liberating and energizing for students. The volumes that some students write are simply astounding because they are excited to share their ideas and to receive feedback. They write out of personal commitment and interest; the genuine purpose for communicating their convictions provides intrinsic motivation for the task.

There are certainly logistical problems that teachers need to solve in using journals. One immediate reaction among teachers is "It's a great idea, but I don't have the time." One solution is to collect journals infrequently, perhaps every few weeks. Another solution is to have students exchange their journals with one another to read and comment on the reflections of their peers. A third alternative is to have a conference about some of the journal entries so that teachers can write brief comments about the journals, rather than lengthy responses. Because the focus is clearly on students' reflections and understanding, teachers may not need to write a great deal or very often to make journals effective for students.

Self-portraits provide another way for students to reflect on themselves and can be provided in letters that students write—to their parents, teachers, friends, or themselves. Teachers typically use three kinds of letters for this purpose. The first is penpal letters in which students exchange information about themselves and their lives with someone else. The activity provides an authentic purpose for writing, practice with a distinct genre, and opportunities to reflect on the personal characteristics and qualities of the writer. A second example

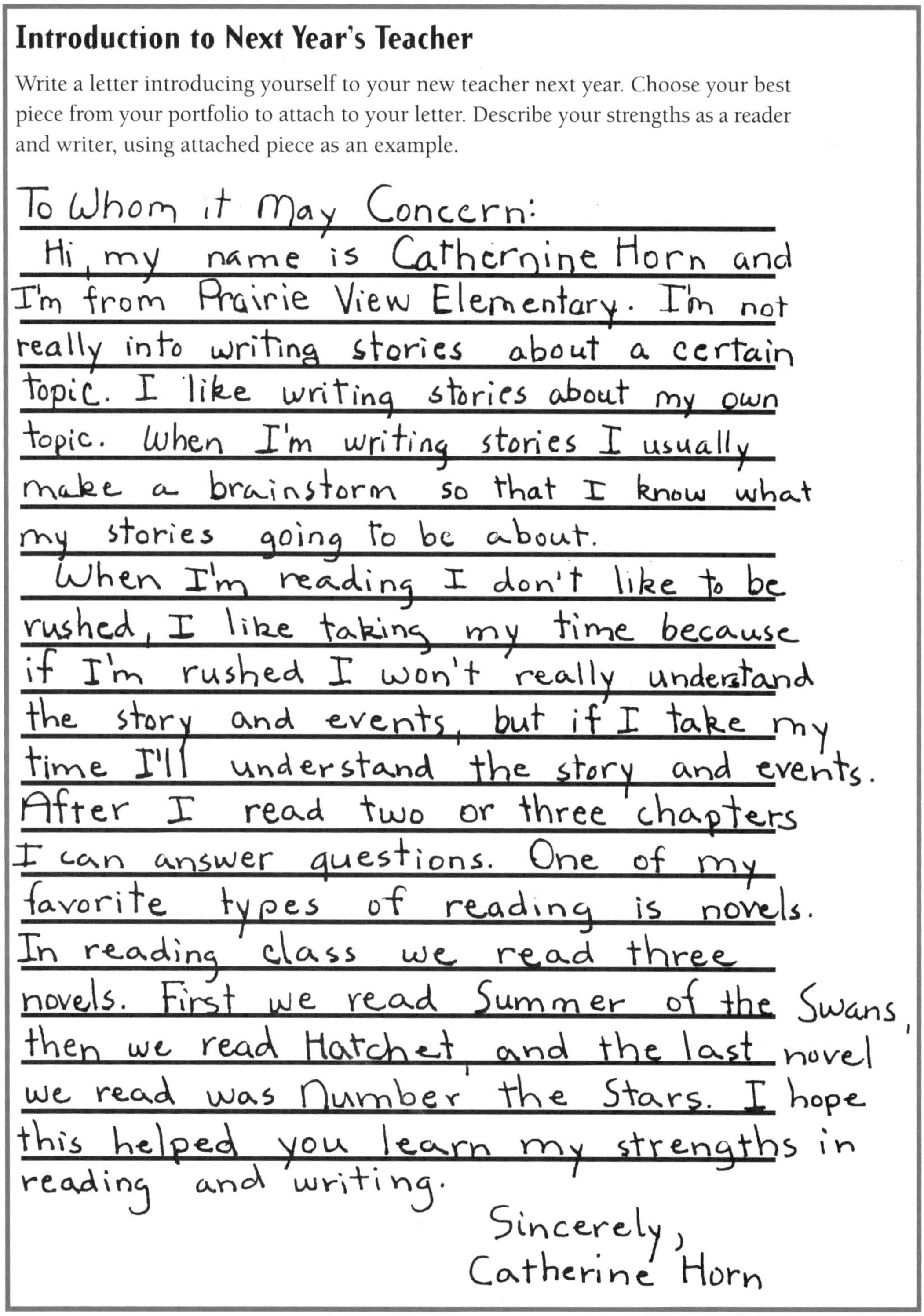

Introduction to Next Year's Teacher

Write a letter introducing yourself to your new teacher next year. Choose your best piece from your portfolio to attach to your letter. Describe your strengths as a reader and writer, using attached piece as an example.

To Whom it May Concern:

Hi, my name is Cathernine Horn and I'm from Prairie View Elementary. I'm not really into writing stories about a certain topic. I like writing stories about my own topic. When I'm writing stories I usually make a brainstorm so that I know what my stories going to be about.

When I'm reading I don't like to be rushed, I like taking my time because if I'm rushed I won't really understand the story and events, but if I take my time I'll understand the story and events. After I read two or three chapters I can answer questions. One of my favorite types of reading is novels. In reading class we read three novels. First we read Summer of the Swans, then we read Hatchet, and the last novel we read was Number the Stars. I hope this helped you learn my strengths in reading and writing.

Sincerely,
Catherine Horn

Figure 11: *A fifth-grader's letter to her future teacher.*

is the letters that students may write to their parents. For example, before a parent–teacher conference, students often wrote letters home to their parents about the kinds of things they had been doing in school and the kinds of things parents should expect to see in the portfolios. Teachers stimulated children to reflect on their accomplishments, their work, and their talents in their letters.

A third type of self-portrait is provided in students' letters to future teachers. We have included an example (see Figure 11) to show how students use letter writing as a vehicle to examine their interests, achievements, and positive characteristics. This provides a fascinating glimpse into children's perceptions of themselves that is useful for future teachers and a wonderful record of their childhood that will be appreciated by parents and the children when they look back on these letters. The collection of letters that students write over the years is another excellent reason for keeping Home Portfolios.

CONFERENCES

We use the term *conference* to describe a purposeful dialogue between two or more people. The underlying goal of most academic conferences is to help the participants gain insight into the motives, learning processes, and standards surrounding one's performance. Insight is more critical than evaluation because productive conferences are mutually informative rather than authoritative. Teachers can use conferences to help students discover their strengths and weaknesses, to appraise progress, and to make reasonable plans for future efforts. Why do conferences elicit personal reflections? Graves (1983) wrote that it is because "children don't know what they know. Most learners don't. When we speak, or when someone elicits information from us, it is as informative to the speaker as it is to the listener" (p. 138). Although conferences vary in purpose, they share the intent of raising students' awareness of their learning and encouraging them to move toward greater self-sufficiency and control.

Graves emphasized the importance of oral language in the curriculum and the effect it can have on a student's understanding. Most children come to our schools with well-developed verbal communication that allows them to express complicated messages orally that they cannot express in written form. Talking with others—expressing ideas verbally—encourages reflectivity by slowing down thinking processes and making them shared. It allows students to test ideas and explore their attitudes. It is important, therefore, that a student's daily classroom experience involve opportunities for self-expression such as conferences. This section describes two kinds of conferences that are typical in schools today, student–teacher conferences and student–student (peer) conferences. Later, we will discuss traditional parent–teacher conferences and how students may participate in those more actively.

> Conferences increase students' awareness of what they know and what they need to work on; they provide metacognitive and motivational information.

Student-Teacher Conferences

The student–teacher conference is an important component in many curricular areas. During these conferences, students talk about their ideas and work while teachers listen and provide feedback. Many of these conferences revolve around students' written work. In the last decade, this has become an important component of the process approach to writing. When students explain and explore the ideas that they have tried to express in writing, both student and teacher may understand better where the intentions were realized and where they fell short. "Children discover both new information, and the personal satisfaction that goes with knowing something, when they hear the information from their own mouths. Best of all there is an audience present to mirror the child's knowing" (Graves, 1983, p. 138). During the conference, the teacher is the audience reflecting the child's "knowing"; however, conferences are also designed for students to reflect on their own "knowing." Revision, a crucial aspect of thinking for every writer, can be fostered with the feedback and self-analysis generated in a conference.

Although the writing conference is widely accepted, teachers use conferences to promote students' self-assessment across the curriculum. For example, when students and teachers discuss the contents of portfolios, they examine a broad range of evidence for progress on multiple dimensions. During a portfolio conference, students and teachers review the artifacts collected from previous weeks as students reflect on what they have learned, and together they set goals for the immediate future. Teachers guide students through the process by emphasizing strengths and areas where the student has exhibited progress. They also help students recognize areas that require improvement. Teachers provide "scaffolding," or temporary assistance erected to support the students' independence, to show students what they need to be doing on their own. Thus, self-assessment is modeled and practiced with teachers on an interpersonal plane and then internalized by students on a personal level (Rogoff, 1990; Vygotsky, 1978).

Teachers might start the portfolio conference by asking students to sift through the contents and explain why these samples are important and what they show. Teachers may want to provide students with a Portfolio Conference Planning Guide similar to the one shown below to structure the conference.

Portfolio Conference Planning Guide

1. What kinds of work do you have in your portfolio?
2. Which piece are you most pleased with? Why?
3. Which piece did you work the hardest on? Why?
4. Which piece would you like to work more on if you could? Why?
5. Comments from your conference partner.

The Conference Planning Guide helps students prepare for their meetings with teachers and offers a starting point for discussion about the students' work. One teacher asked students to complete worksheets titled "Preconference Reflections" that included questions such as "What have I learned?" and "What do I want to learn?" in various subjects. The worksheets helped to stimulate students' analyses before talking with teachers. The success of the conference depends partly on students' expectations and preparation for the conference. We have seen conferences fail when students are confused about the purpose of conferences or when they do not review their work and reactions beforehand.

The conference should include questions about the student's reading and writing strategies, such as "How did you get the ideas for writing this?" "Did you have anyone read your writing and give you suggestions?" and "How did you change it?" These kinds of questions allow students to focus on the actual work in the portfolio so that they can describe the strategies they used or should have used. This is better than vague questions about what "good writers" do because nonspecific questions may elicit answers that students think teachers want to hear, rather than answers based on students' own experiences. Teachers may also want to ask students about their attributions and emotional reactions to work so that they can determine if satisfaction and frustration are interpreted appropriately by students. These questions can tap different kinds of motivational and affective perceptions, such as

☐ Effort and difficulty: "What was the hardest part about reading this book?"

☐ Independent reading and writing: "Which of these things did you read or write just for fun?"

☐ Recognition of genre: "Show me the different kinds of books that you are reading and tell me how they are different."

☐ Self-evaluation: "What things should we work on together this week to help you read and write better?"

☐ Attributions: "Why do you think you did so well (poorly) on this work?"

☐ Satisfaction: "Which of these things makes you feel proud? Which would you like to show your parents? Why?"

Conferences underscore the authenticity of students' work. They give students an audience and a range of purposes for their efforts. They provide teachers with valuable insight about the strengths, needs, and perceptions of the students in the classroom. Both teachers and students use conferences to become more reflective about their performance and to make mutual accommodations in their efforts and strategies. The outcomes of the conference should be recorded. In our project, we provided teachers with a Summary Sheet for students and teachers to write comments. This is shown in Figure 12 and was kept in the portfolios to be used with report cards and parent conferences.

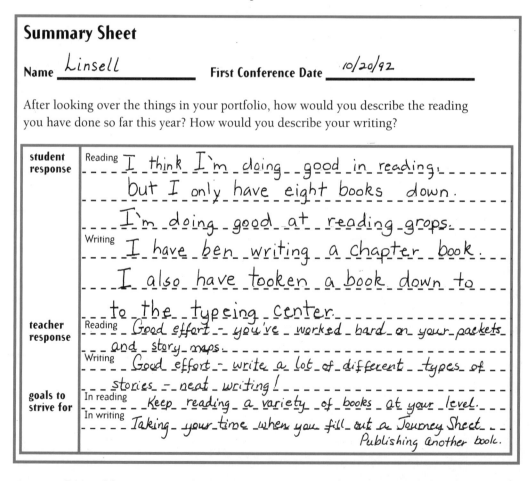

Summary Sheet

Name _Linsell_   **First Conference Date** _10/20/92_

After looking over the things in your portfolio, how would you describe the reading you have done so far this year? How would you describe your writing?

student response	Reading	I think I'm doing good in reading, but I only have eight books down. I'm doing good at reading grops.
	Writing	I have ben writing a chapter book. I also have tooken a book down to to the typeing center.
teacher response	Reading	Good effort -- you've worked hard on your packets and story maps.
	Writing	Good effort -- write a lot of different types of stories -- neat writing!
goals to strive for	In reading	Keep reading a variety of books at your level.
	In writing	Taking your time when you fill out a Journey Sheet. Publishing another book.

Figure 12: *An example of a summary sheet used in a student–teacher conference.*

Peer Conferences

Peer conferences offer opportunities for students to respond to each other's work and discuss their reactions in a nonevaluative manner. When peers confer, they must take on reciprocal roles of author and audience, as explainer and listener, so that the conference builds students' knowledge about both roles of assessment. They become better listeners and better self-assessors when they discuss their work and reconsider it in new perspectives. This is easily observed in peer conferences about writing and revising.

When two students meet to talk about their writing, each author gets a fresh perspective from the conference partner. Questions are asked that serve to clarify areas of the draft that may have been perfectly clear to the author but not so clear to the audience. Young writers typically wander through a first draft taking diversions that might have seemed compelling at the time of the writing but that have little to do with the subject. A conference partner with an objective view will notice the inconsistencies that do not make sense. Through the verbal dialogue of the peer conference, students are forced to focus more clearly on their main points, their organization of ideas, and the clarity of expression (Calkins, 1986).

> Conferences provide an audience and an authentic purpose for reviewing and assessing one's work.

Successful peer conferences do not just happen. They must be planned carefully and orchestrated by the teacher to ensure that each child is aware of his or her particular role in the conference setting, has adequate guidelines to follow, knows what to expect from his or her partner, and knows what to expect from the conference itself. Each small task within the conference situation must be taught, with expectations and standards prescribed. If a conference procedure has been carefully engineered by an insightful teacher who takes steps to promote respectful treatment among students, then the peer conference is a powerful device for promoting self-reflection.

One concrete method that we like to use is worksheets to guide students' writing conferences. Appendix H at the end of the chapter shows the worksheets for a "Blue Dragon" conference that helps students revise a preliminary draft. (This teacher also used a "Yellow Dragon" worksheet to promote editing for technical accuracy.) The "Blue Dragon" conference is aimed at revising and constructing meaning that is sensible to a partner. The guidelines and peer conferences are props intended to support the internalization of these writing skills. We think they are quite valuable for young children. Research has shown that peer conference guidelines can enhance the quality of children's writing (Raphael & Englert, 1990).

Conferences must be practiced in order to be effective; they must become part of the classroom culture by virtue of familiarity rather than short-term explicit training. In Australia, it is not unusual to observe 5- to 6-year-olds writing together and having conferences as they review each others' stories. As you might expect, conferences with young writers are often more amusing than productive, but the hidden value is the developmental foundation that is laid for using peers as resources for learning. By the time Australian children are 8 to 9 years old, process writing conferences are so routine that they are used effectively and independently by most students. When conferences among peers are used successfully for writing and revising, it is a small step to use them throughout the curriculum. For example, self-reflection is also enhanced when students discuss their portfolios with peers. After reviewing the work in their portfolios, students may work in small groups or pairs taking turns describing their work to each other, indicating how it is organized, describing their favorite pieces, and stating reasons for their preferences. Many teachers in Walled Lake schools use a "Classroom Portfolio Day" to encourage students to talk with each other about their work. This is often the first opportunity for students to review their work with someone else, so it is important to set a tone of sharing rather than evaluating each others' work.

Peer conferences can also lead to more public exhibits of students' work. Some teachers let students take turns explaining their best work on Portfolio Days. Others emphasize "Showcase Portfolios," which might be displays in the classroom or hallways. Such exhibits are perfect for parent–teacher conferences, Parent–Teacher Association exhibits, Learning Fairs, and other school-wide activities that demonstrate the achievements of students. All of these exhibits can combine peer conferences and student–teacher conferences with other forms of self-assessment in authentic and meaningful ways.

1 **Reflecting:** Look back through some of the examples of student inventories and self-evaluations illustrated in this chapter. Choose several (or modify them as necessary) to use with your students. Collect students' responses to the inventories and discuss them in class.

2 **Responding:** Create a matrix of different kinds of evidence that can be gathered to support the judgments that teachers make on report cards. Enter several of the most important features of literacy included on the report card and then identify what kinds of performance, process, and perception evidence you use that is relevant to each feature.

	Reading	Writing	Speaking/Listening
Evidence:			
Performance			
Process			
Perception			

3 **Sharing:** Take the inventories and self-evaluations that you chose in "Reflecting" above and share them with another teacher at your grade level. If you did not choose any, show him or her some of the examples and ask if he or she uses anything like them and whether or not they have been useful.

4 **Reviewing:** The purpose of this chapter is to provide a framework for teachers to examine their existing assessment practices in order to identify areas that may not be assessed adequately. We have found that the report card categories are useful starting points for the matrix of assessment evidence, but teachers may not be satisfied with the dimensions highlighted on report cards. Part of assessment reform is the realignment of the evidence that teachers collect with the public reports that they make. This ensures that we do not continue to report minor parts of the curriculum nor omit evidence for the features that really count. A sample of a matrix is provided in Figure 13 that fourth grade teachers constructed at a workshop.

Assessment Measures	Areas of Assessment											When Collected
	Language Arts - Reading					Language Arts - Writing						
	Puts forth effort	Reads independently	Demonstrates comprehension	Uses word strategies	Recognizes literary elements	Writes for a variety of purposes	Develops topic/draft	Revises content	Demonstrates language/grammar	Applies spelling/daily use	Writes legibly	
Performances												
QRI	✓		✓	✓								
Taped Readings	✓		✓	✓								
Final Drafts						✓	✓	✓	✓	✓	✓	
Processes												
Story Maps	✓		✓		✓							
KWL	✓		✓									
Prewriting and Rough Drafts	✓					✓	✓	✓	✓			
Reader Response		✓	✓	✓	✓							
Perceptions												
Parent Survey	✓	✓				✓						
Journal Entries	✓	✓				✓			✓	✓		
Inventories	✓											

Figure 13: *A worksheet for teachers to use in identifying the match between evidence of students' learning and areas of assessment.*

STUDENT'S & PARENT'S REFLECTIONS

Student's Name _____ **Parent's Name** _____

☐ Take a guided tour through the portfolio and identify 3 pieces of good work from different areas of the curriculum. Discuss why you like each one.

	Student Choices	**Parent Choices**
1.		
2.		
3.		

☐ Talk with each other about some aspect of the portfolio that makes you very proud.

Student Selection	**Parent Selection**

☐ In the next few months I'm going to try to improve performance at school by ...

Student Goal	**Parent Goal**

Student's signature _____ Parent's signature _____

Date _____

READING ATTITUDE INVENTORY

Name _____ **Date** _____

	😊	😐	😮
1. How do you feel when your teacher reads a story out loud?			
2. How do you feel when someone gives you a book for a present?			
3. How do you feel about reading books for fun at home?			
4. How do you feel when you are asked to read out loud to your group?			
5. How do you feel when you are asked to read out loud to the teacher?			
6. How do you feel when you are asked to read out loud to a friend?			
7. How do you feel when you come to a new word while reading?			
8. How do you feel when it is time to do your worksheet?			
9. How do you feel about going to school?			
10. How do you feel about going to Chapter 1?			
11. How do you see yourself as a reader?			
12. How do you think your teacher sees you as a reader?			
13. How do you feel about the reading group you are in?			
14. How do you feel about writing?			
15. How do you feel about reading a book when you get to choose the book?			
Total			

ATTITUDES ABOUT READING

Name _____ **Date** _____

1. What kinds of books do you like to read at home?

   _____

   _____

   _____

2. Complete this sentence in your own words.

   I think reading is _____

   _____

   _____

3. Read each sentence below. Do you agree with what it says? Circle you opinion
   after each sentence.

I like to read to learn new things.	Yes	No	Not Sure
Reading books is kind of boring.	Yes	No	Not Sure
Sometimes I relax by reading.	Yes	No	Not Sure
Reading is important to me.	Yes	No	Not Sure
I like to read magazines.	Yes	No	Not Sure
Reading is really hard for me.	Yes	No	Not Sure
I like to help other kids read.	Yes	No	Not Sure

| APPENDIX D | A self-assessment of writing processes for the fifth grade.

STUDENT WRITING SURVEY

Name _____ **Date** _____

1. Do you think of yourself as a writer? Tell me why.

2. How did you learn to write?

3. Does your teacher think you're a writer?

4. What does your teacher think is a good piece of writing?

5. What do you write about?

6. Where do you get your ideas for writing?

7. Do you like to write alone or with a friend?

| **APPENDIX E** | A self-assessment of spelling processes for the fifth grade. |

SPELLING INTERVIEW

Name _____ **Grade** _____ **Date** _____

1. Are you a good speller? _____

   Why do you think so?

   _____

   _____

   _____

2. What makes someone a good speller?

   _____

   _____

   _____

3. What do you do when you don't know how to spell a word?

   _____

   _____

   _____

4. If someone is having trouble spelling a word how could you help that person?

   _____

   _____

   _____

HOW I SEE MYSELF AS A READER

Name _____   **Date** _____

		T	F
Choosing My Books			
I usually choose books that I can read easily.		_____	_____
I like to read different kinds of books.		_____	_____
If my friend tells me about a good book, I usually read it.		_____	_____
Reading on My Own			
I like silent reading time in school.		_____	_____
I like to read books my teacher has read aloud.		_____	_____
I read at home.		_____	_____
Talking About Books			
I enjoy talking about books I've read.		_____	_____
I usually understand what I read.		_____	_____
I know how to check back in the book to support my answers.		_____	_____
Book Activities			
I write in my Reading Log when I complete a book.		_____	_____
I enjoy working on book projects with others.		_____	_____
I enjoy reading with a friend.		_____	_____

Students' reflections and goal setting can be encouraged by teachers' questions.

SEMESTER REFLECTIONS

Name _____ **Date** _____

☐ Think about all the projects and work you've done so far this year. What do you think is the most important thing you have learned?

Would you like to know more about it?

☐ What has been the most unusual thing you've learned?

Why?

☐ What are you looking forward to learning next semester?

Why?

REVISING SHEET

Name _____

Conference partner's name _____

You will need a red pencil for this part of your writing. Get one from the writing center. Please return it when you finish.

____ 1. Choose a draft you would like to publish.

____ 2. Read your draft to a friend. Ask your friend what he or she likes best about your draft. Record you friend's comments here:

_____

_____

_____

____ 3. Think about your partner's suggestions. Work on your draft again. See if you can use some of your friend's ideas in your story.

____ 4. Have a *Blue Dragon* Conference with a friend. Use your Revising Dragon to help you. Try to improve your draft's beginning and ending. Be sure it has good sentence order and that it *makes sense* to your friend.

____ 5. Put your draft in Conference Box 1 for a Revising Conference with your teacher.

____ 6. Recopy your draft after our conference.

(continued on next page)

EDITING SHEET

Name _____

Conference partner's name _____

You will need a red pencil for this part of your writing. Get one from the writing center. Please return it when you finish.

_____ 1. Circle all the words you think are misspelled. Correct as many as you can.

_____ 2. Make sure all of your sentences begin with a capital letter and end with some kind of punctuation.

_____ 3. Be sure your sentences are *complete sentences* (with a subject and a predicate).

_____ 4. Do you have any sentences that are *more* than a sentence should be?

_____ 5. Did you capitalize all proper nouns? Remember—those are the names of people, places, and things.

_____ 6. Did you indent each new paragraph?

_____ 7. Have a *Yellow Dragon* Conference with a friend. Use your yellow proof-reading dragons to help you.

_____ 8. Recopy your draft if it is hard to read.

_____ 9. Put your draft in Conference Box 2 for an Editing Conference with your teacher.

(continued on next page)

REVISING DRAGON

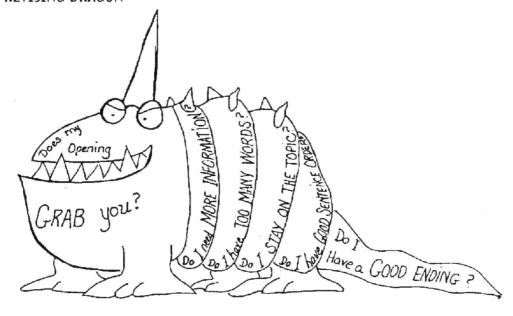

PROOFREADING DRAGON

SUGGESTED READINGS

Hill, B. C., & Ruptic, C. A. (1994). *Practical aspects of authentic assessment.* Norwood, MA: Christopher-Gordon.

Perrone, V. (Ed.). (1991). *Expanding student assessment.* Alexandria, VA: Association for Supervision and Curriculum Development.

Rhodes, L. K. (1993). *Literacy assessment: A handbook of instruments.* Portsmouth, NH: Heinemann.

Tierney, R. J., Carter, M. A., & Desai, L. E. (1991). *Portfolio assessment in the reading-writing classroom.* Norwood, MA: Christopher-Gordon.

goal four

Strengthening Home-School
Connections

"**School life should grow gradually out of the home life ... it should take up and continue the activities with which the child is already familiar in the home.**" John Dewey

Although the title of this book emphasizes the processes by which students become reflective on their own learning and teachers become reflective on their own practices, we believe it is equally important for parents to reflect on their roles in the education of their children. Many parents wish that the lines of communication with teachers were more open and more frequent. Sometimes the problems are institutional barriers, sometimes they are consequences of parents and teachers who are too busy or disorganized, and sometimes the good intentions just never seem to be carried out. Whatever the source of communication difficulties between home and school, we believe that parents and teachers can provide valuable information about children that will promote their education if they are given opportunities to share their insights with each other. In this section, we would like to present information about six different avenues of communication that can be used by both teachers and parents to become more reflective about children.

LETTERS

The most common form of communication among teachers and parents is a simple letter. Parents often use letters to inform teachers about special needs or conditions of their children, whereas teachers often use letters to communicate impending events such as field trips or class projects. Letters can also provide valuable information about classroom practices. One teacher in California devised a letter for her first-graders during the first week of school, shown below, to solicit parents' help in selecting suitable books to assess children's oral reading. While listening to each student read, she kept a running record of the oral reading miscues and took a few notes about the child's reading. She shared these observations with parents at the first conference. It was also at this time that she explained her views on emergent literacy, spelling approximations, making reasonable guesses about words in text, and the need to read real books in the first grade.

> Dear Parents,
>
> To help me get to know your child better, I'll be listening to your child read aloud. Please help your child select a book, poem, or some other short text that they wish to share with me. Please help your child practice reading the selection at home before bringing it to school in the next week or two.
>
> Sincerely,

Mrs. Carallano, another dynamic first-grade teacher in Michigan, uses letters to inform parents about her focus on emergent literacy. She describes their daily Writers' Workshop, in which children draw a picture on the top half of a page and write about it on the bottom. She calms parents' apprehension about their children's invented spelling as she provides background information for her writing activities. She explains that the children's daily compositions go into their portfolios, the best one is selected each Friday to keep in the portfolio, and the others are taken home for the Home Portfolios.

Other teachers use letters to engage parents in their children's school activities. For example, Mrs. Fitzgerald, a sixth-grade teacher, used a letter to notify families that the topography assignments were due in five days. To make sure that parents helped their children to meet the deadline, she asked parents to ask their children one question, write the answer, sign the letter, and return it to the teacher. This simple procedure made the parents aware of the childrens' assignment and made them partly responsible for the completion of the assignment by the deadline.

Dear Family,

The topography assignments are due in only FIVE (5) DAYS! I have been checking children's logs every week to see how they are doing and to answer any questions that they might have. So far we have 2 students who have completed the project! (You may bring them in anytime.)

The purpose of this hands-on assignment is to complement the reading we are doing about geographical features. Please write your child's answer to the following question and return this form to me by March 22nd. Thank you.

The most interesting aspect of China's topography that I learned is:

_____

_____

Parent's signature _____ Date _____

Student's signature _____ Date _____

In another example, Joanie Moore used the children's monthly Book Logs to tell parents about the variety of genres the children would read in the following month; fairy tales, poems, mysteries, and magazines (see Figures 14a and 14b). Children were required to record the date, the title, and the author of books they had read in their logs, but they were also required to check off the different examples of various genres on the form. Providing this basic information to parents informed them of Mrs. Moore's classroom procedures as well as the variety of books that their children were reading. Rather than keeping the information at school, the teacher shared it with parents in a simple form letter.

Mrs. Moore used similar forms in her third grade to share periodic evaluations with parents. For example, she used an animal report form to communicate with parents her evaluation of one class project. Every student in her class chose a different animal to study. They were required to create a book based on their investiga-

November Book Log

Name **Jody**

No.	Date	Title	Author
1	11-6-93	McBroom tells a lie	Sid Fleishman
2	11-11-93	Ralph .S. Mouse	Beverly Cleary
3	11-11-93	Love you Forever	Robert Munch
4	11-12-93	Animals Animals	Eric carle
5	11-12-93	Old turtles Riddle and Joke book	Leonard Kessler
6	11-12-93	the kids cat book	Tomie DePaola
7	11-12-93	The good luck christmas tree	Ursula Moray Williams
8	11-15-93	Slue-foot sue and Pecos Bil	Robert D Sansoucil
9	11-16-93	little bears thanksgiving	Janice
10	11-21-93	Old Stormalong: The deep water sailor	Robert D Sansoucil
11	11-29-93	How my parents learned to eat	Ina R Friedman
12	12-1-93	a kiss for little bear	Else Holmelund Minarik
13	12-1-93	The Riddles	Benard Wiseman
14	12-1-93	Large as life daytime Animals	Joanna cole
15	12-1-93	Large as life nighttime Animals	Joanna cole
16	12-5-93	Charlotte's web	E.B White
17	12-6-93	I hate English!	Ellen Levine
18			
19			
20			

Figure 14a: *An example of a monthly Book Log.*

November Book Log

Dear Parents,
During the month of November your child will need to complete these requirements:

        ☑☑ 2 Fairy Tales
        ☑ 1 Poetry
      ☑☑☑ 3 Non-fiction
       ☑☑ 2 Chapter Books
        ☑ 1 Mystery (Fiction)
       ☑☑ 2 Picture Books
        ☑ 1 Children's Magazine (Fiction or Non-fiction)
     ☑☑☑ 3 Others of his/her choice

The Book Log form (see attached) is to be returned each Friday. Your child can record the books he/she has read throughout the week on his/her Book Log at school. Thank you for your cooperation.

Figure 14b: *An example of a monthly Book Log.*

tions and to give oral reports. The teacher evaluated each child's research, book, and oral presentation. These comments were recorded for the child's feedback but also sent home so the parent could sign and return the form. This letter was then placed in the child's portfolio.

Just as letters allow teachers and parents to express their respect and appreciation for each other, they can be used for the same purpose with students. Mr. Morrison regularly encouraged parents to write letters to their children and leave them on the student's desk to be discovered the following day. Another teacher encouraged parents to enclose letters or notes in their children's lunch boxes. Sometimes parents write letters to their children following a parent–teacher conference. At other times, the letters are simple expressions of affection, such as this letter from a mother to her daughter:

Dearest Michelle,

I am so proud of you! You continue to do fantastic work! I can tell you're trying very hard, and it's paying off. I know it's hard for you with me working so hard and such long hours. Your efforts at home and at school are helping our family and you to grow. Let's keep finding special times to spend together, I love them!

I am so happy you have been involved in school activities like "Say No to Drugs" and "Peacemakers." They're not only fun but show everyone that you're very interested in making your life and others peaceful and beautiful and very rewarding. You've grown up so much, but you're still my little girl. I can't think of anything you need to work on. Just keep doing what you're doing, and be happy.

I love you, Mom.

Letters are informal and quick means to build personal relationships. Parents can express their insights and appreciation in notes to teachers. Whether jotted on a scrap of paper or on stationery, the letters reveal that parents were involved in their children's schoolwork because of the teachers' activities that made them partners. Parents reacted positively to reviewing their children's performance; they found it informative and helpful. These little notes go a long way toward improving the communication and mutual respect between teachers and parents. Here are two examples:

Jeanie,

I really enjoyed going over the reading packet with Lindsey. What a thorough and informative way of assessing her skills and finding the areas where she needs more help.

Kim

Dear Mrs. A,

Barbara and I are very appreciative of your efforts last year with our daughter Ellen. She thrived under your guidance and enthusiastically pursued her studies. You slaked her thirst for learning. We are very appreciative of you—your interest, leadership, and enthusiasm.

Sincerely, J.A.

P.S. Please think of Ellen whenever you see an ore carrier.

The second letter has special significance for this book's second author because the father who wrote the letter had been an active participant in her third-grade class. Although he was a busy executive, he had made a lively presentation to the class about the ships that carry ore throughout the Great Lakes. He had become a participant in the classroom and developed a relationship with students and the teacher that extended beyond his own daughter's interests. His understanding and appreciation of the teacher's efforts are reflected in his brief note.

PARENTS' PROFILES OF THEIR CHILDREN

Teachers can solicit a great deal of information from parents that can be used to construct "profiles" of their children's habits and interests. The information can facilitate how and what teachers do in the classroom. Teachers may ask parents about topics of interest, study habits, literacy practice, television viewing habits, library visits, and homework routines of children. This information is often vital to teachers, who find out what kinds of encouragement and support children receive at home. One first-grade teacher, Mrs. King, begins the year by asking parents to share information about their children's literacy. The questions simply ask in a yes/no format if children are interested in school, if they retell stories, if they enjoy music and art, if they respond to environmental print, and so forth. Such forms can be filled out quickly by parents and noted informally by teachers. It is easy to put these in a child's portfolio for later reference.

A slightly different parent survey used by a second-grade teacher, Mrs. Sullivan, asked parents to describe children's reactions when books are read aloud to them, the kinds of books and magazines their children prefer, and how children feel about themselves as readers and writers (see Figure 15). These questions ask parents to probe the psychological reactions of their children to literacy and school and to share those reactions with the teachers. In this manner, teachers can use profiles of students to make initial instructional decisions about literacy levels and literacy interests. Of course, teachers and parents can communicate about children's changing interests throughout the year, so it is a good idea to request such profiles from parents periodically. Parents reflect on their children as they fill out these surveys, just as teachers reflect on children's backgrounds and experiences as they read them. The end result is that all participants know more about the children and share the information with each other.

PARENT-TEACHER CONFERENCES

Parent–teacher conferences are a mainstay of American schools, typically occurring once or twice during the year, often coinciding with the issuance of report cards. They are usually attended by one or both parents, and they almost always follow a plan designed by teachers. Parent–teacher conferences offer familiar avenues for teachers to communicate about students' performance in school. Some parents are eager to attend conferences, and some parents are not. Indeed, many teachers are frustrated by parents' nonattendance at school conferences and their reluctance in becoming involved with their children's education. We believe that conferences can be threatening to parents for many reasons. Sometimes parents are ashamed about their children's lack of progress, sometimes parents themselves are intimidated by teachers and schools, sometimes they do not understand enough of the work that the child has been doing to offer reactions or ask questions, and sometimes they are frustrated by teachers who, they feel, "do not understand" their children. We believe that part

Parent Survey

Name _____   Grade _____

Parent _____   Date _____

1. Does your child enjoy being read to?

2. What is your child's favorite book or magazine?

3. Does your child write at home? Please describe the kinds of writing your child engages in most often.

4. How does your child feel about school?

5. What would you like me to know about your child's reading

6. What else would you like me to know about your child?

Figure 15: *An example of a parent survey of children's literacy habits and attitudes.*

of the solution to problems of parent–teacher communication is finding better ways to inform parents about their children's progress during the parent–teacher conference. Here are two suggestions.

One way to improve parent–teacher conferences is to base the conference on a review of the student's work that is meaningful and sensible to the parent. That is why we have found portfolios so valuable. If parents have been informed about work throughout the school year and have received copies of children's schoolwork, then the parents are more likely to understand the projects and activities that teachers discuss. A focus on a review of work is facilitated when teachers do not emphasize test scores, relative placement in a class, ability grouping, or grade-level equivalent curriculum materials. These pieces of information tend to stratify children by ability and do not focus on the unique talents and individual progress of children. Parents want to know that their children are working hard, progressing well, and learning important information. This is most easily satisfied by showing parents tangible examples of children's work, such as the books they have read, the papers they have written, and the projects they have completed. The following letter was written by a mother to her daughter following a parent–teacher conference in which portfolios were central:

> Dear Tash,
>
> I am so proud of your report card. All A's. You have put forth a lot of effort this semester in your work and it shows. You went up in a lot of the application areas and this shows you are really striving to do better. It makes me proud that you work so hard and care about school so much.
>
> I enjoy looking through all your papers and seeing the good grades. I know it makes you proud of yourself. I would like to read all of your stories. And the comic you drew was wonderful.

I think Michelle and Mrs. H. were right—it did deserve all 3's! Keep up the good work.

Love, Mom.

Even among students in junior high and secondary school, comparative ability measures such as standardized test scores and grades should not be the primary focus of parent–teacher conferences about children. Such a focus mistakenly elevates these outcomes, rather than knowledge, motivation, and effective learning strategies, as fundamental goals of schooling. When parents focus only on improving test scores, their roles as partners in education are diminished. They can exhort their children to try harder and to practice taking tests, but not much else. This outcome is typical in Japan, where many children attend "cram schools" at night to practice taking tests and where "education moms" constantly demand greater efforts and achievements from their children (Stevenson & Stigler, 1992). In contrast, conferences allow parents and teachers opportunities to focus on students' growth and their unique accomplishments. Parents feel satisfied when they believe that teachers understand their children as individuals and when teachers are knowledgeable about children's development. For example, one parent wrote the following letter after her conference with her daughter's third-grade teacher:

Dear Mrs. Ayres,

My conference with you last week was the most rewarding and insightful one I have ever had. Just glimpsing how you teach, analyze and evaluate is exciting! I am encouraging Katie to slow down and do her work more carefully and neatly. We will work on "transferring" knowledge, too.

Thank you for such a valuable experience. I can see why Katie is enjoying this year with you. Best wishes for a lovely Thanksgiving, D.F.

A second suggestion to improve conferences is to invite students to participate. We have worked with many teachers who have asked students to lead the parent conference by reviewing their own work. Before the conference, children examine the contents of their portfolios and select pieces of their work that represent their accomplishments during the past few months. In other words, they review and reflect on their work in order to prepare what they present and say to their parents. Children provide descriptions of their schoolwork to their parents as they explain what it is, why they did it, and why they are proud of it. Students are given the responsibility and authority to review and assess their own performance with their parent and teacher as the audience. This dissolves tension between teachers and parents, provides a focus on the students' interpretation of their own schoolwork, and provides a meaningful purpose for students to be reflective. Student-led conferences can be held once or twice a year and provide wonderful opportunities to help students take control of their own learning while informing their parents. In these conferences, all of the participants can take pride in children's accomplishments. Teachers who choose to involve students in parent–teacher conferences confirm that children know a great deal about their learning and can provide insights into their own development.

The following letter was written from a parent who had just participated in a three-way conference led by her daughter. The letter clearly expresses her pride in her daughter's poise and achievement.

> Dear Emily,
>
> It was a pleasure having you with me at your conference. You handled yourself well. Your father and I could not be prouder! Your hard work is obvious on your report card.
>
> Keep up the hard work, Emy! Your enthusiasm and pride in your work comes through loud and clear and that is most important.
>
> Love, Mom.

HOME PORTFOLIOS

The conferences, letters, and parent profiles can all be enhanced by the use of Home Portfolios. We have observed a number of teachers use Home Portfolios with great success. For example, in Walled Lake Schools, where we initiated Home Portfolios, parents have been encouraged to create folders to hold their children's work. They are given explanations about the portfolios at school in letters and at PTA meetings so they can replicate the purposes and format of the School Portfolio. At school, teachers collect information about the *performance* of children in various tasks, the *processes* by which they learn, and student's *perceptions* of their own learning. These three kinds of assessments are also linked directly to the report cards. When parents understand these three areas that are emphasized in School Portfolios, they understand the purpose of many classroom assignments.

The Home Portfolios allow a convenient way to store materials that can be reviewed in conferences or at any time with teachers. They also serve as archival storage places for material so that students regard their work as important enough to be shared with the family and saved for the future. The designation "Home Portfolio" formalizes the boxes of odds and ends that many families already collect, but it also is a seductive practice that involves the family in reviewing their children's school performance in an ongoing manner. Many families review work samples and artifacts from their own school days or their children's earlier grades with great enjoyment and satisfaction. Thus, Home Portfolios help to organize and embellish purposes for learning that many families already use.

> Journals between parents and teachers can facilitate communication.

DIALOGUE JOURNALS

Another way to increase parent–teacher communication is to create journals that travel back and forth between school and home. The purpose of a Dialogue Journal, which can be a spiral notebook or similar notepad, is to create an opportunity for periodic commentaries between teachers and parents. When teachers are especially pleased with the child's performance or are especially concerned with some aspect of their development, they can simply write in the Dialogue Journal for parents to read. Children can take these Dialogue Journals home for parents to read and respond, and return them to school. Conversely, when parents want to provide comments to teachers, they can send them in the journals. Dialogue Journals can easily include letters, reports, and parent profiles and could be stored in portfolios at home and school. In other words, Dialogue Journals can overlap with some of our other suggestions and be incorporated into teachers' preferred style of communication.

Exchanging written messages via dialogue journals or notebooks helps teachers and parents avoid the frustration of communication barriers such as lack of telephone access. Nothing is more exasperating for parents or teachers than to waste time leaving telephone messages or having confidential conversations overheard in teachers' lounges or school offices. The Dialogue Journals offer a solution that is convenient and *relatively* private, a qualification because students have access to the journals if they carry them between home and school. The fact that children may read the journals prompts parents and teachers to write comments that will enhance students' reflection. We recognize that teachers do not have time to reply to Dialogue Journals on a daily basis to every parent, but if parents know that this avenue of communication is open, there is always an invitation to "talk" with the teacher.

HOME–SCHOOL CLASSROOM ACTIVITIES

We feel that the best way for parents to become informed about their children's experiences in school is for parents to participate in shared activities. To encourage this kind of interaction, many teachers organize ongoing programs in which parents are involved in a cooperative manner with their child. Some activities of this nature take place at home and others occur in classrooms. They all have the purpose of drawing parents into learning situations with their children that are usually enjoyable for everyone involved. Here are four examples of activities that involve parents in their children's learning.

A Visit From Leo the Lion

One favorite home–school activity that primarily occurs at home has many names because it is so versatile and can be used at several grade levels. We describe it as "A Visit from Leo the Lion" because that is what we observed most recently. The basic activity can be easily modified to suit various ages and interests.

Leo the Lion was introduced to Mrs. Walgreen's first-grade students at the beginning of the year. Before her students entered the classroom, Mrs. Walgreen had placed a small, closed suitcase on her desk. At the children's urging, when they were settled for the morning activities, Mrs. Walgreen opened the suitcase to reveal what was inside. She showed the children a small stuffed animal named Leo the Lion and a variety of objects surrounding him in the suitcase. Leo had a blanket, a toothbrush, a small tube of toothpaste, a comb, and an extra shirt. Next to these items, Mrs. Walgreen had put a large pack of crayons, a set of colored markers, a picture dictionary, and a bound book of blank pages. This, she explained to the children, was Leo's journal. Leo needed a journal so that all of the experiences and adventures he was going to have with his friends could be recorded. When the

> Parents can be involved in classroom learning activities that occur at home.

children looked puzzled, the teacher explained that *they* were Leo's friends who were going to be responsible for Leo's journal. Each night someone in the class would take Leo home in his suitcase. Leo would spend the night with that child in his or her home, and all of the adventures they had together would be recorded in the journal by the child. These journal entries might include descriptions of Leo's evening with the family, such as where he sat at the dinner table, what he ate for dinner, special places he went, where he slept at night, and anything else the child thought would be interesting to record. When they both returned to school the next day, the child would read Leo's journal to his classmates during the morning activities. Leo would then go back into his suitcase and rest for his next adventure, which would begin when he went home with another class member that afternoon.

Mrs. Walgreen's students were excited to hear of Leo's adventures each morning, just as they were motivated to write in Leo's journal each evening. At home, parents were involved in helping their children organize their thoughts and express them in the journal. Some parents added their own comments regarding Leo's behavior while he was visiting or problems he had during the night. Many parents said that they enjoyed reading what other children wrote and seeing the range of text produced by children in the same class.

Comments to the Author

A second activity that enhances the home–school connection involves students' published writing. Many teachers gather writing pieces from every student in the room and compile them in a class book. Mrs. Rubenstein described an activity that enabled her students' parents to read and respond to the student books. Each class book was given a library "check-out" pocket, which students signed before they took the class book home for the evening. The students read the book at home, but in addition, part of the student's responsibility was to have his or her parents write "Comments to the Authors" on the pages in the back of the book included for that purpose. After a few months of circulation, each book contained comments from parents of most of the children in the class. The books become treasures that are read over and over in the classroom library. Parents also enjoy adding comments in their children's individually published books. For students, the value of their written work rises dramatically when parents show appreciation for their efforts.

Independent Reading Programs

Many teachers maintain organized classroom independent reading programs. One teacher explained Rocket Reading, a program that had been successful for her fourth-grade students. Her students were required to keep a reading log of books they had read outside of school. The students were responsible for completing a book slip for each book they read. These book slips were signed by the parents and were placed in the "rocket fuel tank" to be tallied. As an incentive to read consistently, the students set goals for the class to strive for, such as 100 books read, 250 books read, 500 books read, 750 books read, and so on. These goals were displayed as planets taped on the walls around the room. As the class read more and moved toward each goal, the rocket moved to the planet that represented the number of books read. The teacher identified major goals, such as 1,000 books read, as worthy of a class popcorn party. Throughout the year, the children watched their rocket reach goal after goal as they continued to read steadily at home. Parents were continuously involved as they signed book slips for their children and read about the collective progress of the class in weekly newsletters.

Poetry Celebration

A fourth ongoing activity, Class Poetry Celebration, became an important part of Ms. Colson's third-grade classroom and provided a positive vehicle for parent–student–teacher interaction. Ms. Colson explained the program to students and parents at Open House at the beginning of the year. Each Friday afternoon, the students had a Poetry Celebration, at which five to six students would read one of their favorite poems. The children would sign up to be a reader early in the week so they would have time to choose a poem and practice it before the Celebration on Friday. In addition, one parent per week could attend as a guest. The guest parent's responsibility was to begin the Celebration with a selection of poems chosen by the parent and his or her child. Parents and students shared the reading in various ways. Sometimes each would read a poem in its entirety, sometimes they would alternate lines of the same poem, sometimes the child would read a poem that the parent elaborated on to the class, and sometimes the parent would read a poem while the child pantomimed the actions. The choice was left to the participating parent and child. Following the guest reading, students who had signed up and practiced poems during the week had their turns in front of the class. When all poems were read, the class enjoyed refreshments brought by the guest parent and served by the child and several helpers.

Activities such as the Poetry Celebration, A Visit From Leo the Lion, Comments to the Author, and Rocket Reading allow parents to become involved with classroom activities in a substantial, nontrivial way. These activities draw parents into the school experience to enhance their emotional involvement and shared understanding. Teachers who make use of activities such as these enjoy positive relationships with the parents of their students. Parents are able to become part of the classroom culture and thus perceive their children's school experiences in a more meaningful way. As a result, parents are able to reflect on their children's education as well as their own. When they feel a part of the classroom "family," involved throughout the year, parents are more able to understand their children's reactions to school and the purpose of classroom activities. The parent becomes a supporter of the teacher as well as the child.

> Home-school activities that involve parents in substantial, nontrivial ways tend to promote positive relationships among parents, teachers, and students.

All of these options can be adapted and used by teachers and parents to increase communication before marking periods and conferences, so that those assessment opportunities become extensions of an ongoing conversation between teachers and parents about their students' progress. The purpose of these activities is to provide better information, more frequent communication, mutual respect, and greater opportunities to reflect on students' strengths, weaknesses, and progress. When parents are reflective and involved in their students' learning, students become more motivated and teachers are better prepared to offer appropriate instruction.

In summary, we have discussed six avenues to promote increased dialogue between parents and teachers that build positive interpersonal relationships. These avenues are: letters, parents' profiles of their children, parent–teacher conferences, home portfolios, dialogue journals, and home–school classroom activities. The consequences of having supportive relationships between parents and teachers are many. Parents are involved in classroom experiences in meaningful ways, which keeps them informed about their students' progress. This increases their understanding of the issues their children face in their school experiences. Positive, supportive relationships also provide a basis for increased empathy and mutual respect to develop.

Teachers are able to appreciate parents in more personal ways when positive relationships are established. For example, they are aware of the work their children's parents do, as well as their travels, their hobbies, their favorite recipes, their favorite authors, and in some cases, their experiences in school. These little bits of information enhance the work teachers do with their students. Sometimes, these positive relationships can have a profound effect on teachers as well. One personal anecdote from this book's second author illustrates the powerful effect parents can have on teachers when a supportive relationship has been established:

> Renee was a student in my third-grade class several years ago. Shortly after the school year began, I met her father, Dr. B., who was a single parent raising three

children alone. Renee was the "middle child" who did not seem to have the same verve for school that her older sister had. She was still struggling with reading and did not seem to approach her tasks with much delight. Renee's father was very concerned about her progress and adjustment to third grade.

As the year progressed, Renee was very involved with other students in all of our classroom projects. Her reading and writing improved considerably, and she began to blossom socially. I had many conferences with Dr. B. throughout the year to keep him apprised of Renee's progress. During our conversations, his relief and pleasure with her progress was apparent and often intense, which was touching to me. At the end of the year, we were both pleased with her growth in all areas, and Renee was proud of herself and the things she was able to do. Dr. B. was no longer the anxious parent he had been in September, and Renee was leaving my classroom as an excited soon-to-be fourth-grader.

During my last conference with Dr. B., he surprised me by turning the conversation in another direction. He was head of holistic medicine at a large university hospital in the area. He said he had noticed that my style of teaching was similar to his style of practicing medicine because we both considered the social and emotional aspects of our "clients" to be just as important as the main areas of our work, academic instruction in my case and medicine in his case. Our discussion about the similarity of our approaches was very revealing to me because I had never thought of my teaching in that way. His comments have had a lasting effect on me, and I often reflect on them as I examine my convictions about children, parents, and teachers and the supporting relationships we provide for each other.

Dr. B.'s insightful observations could only have resulted from his involvement in our classroom activities and the many conferences we had throughout the year, which developed into a positive, supportive relationship. Although our primary interest at the time was Renee, my conversations with Dr. B. gave me a valuable perspective that has enabled me to reflect on my profession in a different light. I think of Renee and her father often, and the reflections they provoked about my philosophy of teaching.

The positive relationships between parents and teachers clearly benefit students because of the improved communication and shared information. However, as the anecdote above reveals, teachers often reflect on their own professional development and teaching practices because of the experiences of individual parents and students. In the next section, we will explore the kinds of reflections that teachers had as they used portfolios and helped students become more proficient with self-assessment.

1 **Reflecting:** How do you usually communicate with parents about students' progress? Do you think portfolios, letters, and journals can increase parents' involvement with their children's education and inform them about policies and practices at school?

2 **Responding:** Choose one of the methods of communication suggested in this chapter to try with parents at your school. Revise it as needed when you fill out the chart below.

Example for parents	What I like about it is ...	What I would change is ...

3

Sharing: Invite your students to the parent–teacher conference so that the students can lead a discussion of their performance and progress in school. The purpose of this conference is to give students responsibility for explaining their work and evaluating the quality of their performance and effort. The conference promotes students' ownership of their work and pride in their accomplishments.

4

Reviewing: This chapter illustrates how teachers can inform parents about their children's education on a regular and informal basis through portfolios, letters, and other forms of communication. When parents understand the curriculum and what teachers expect students to accomplish, they can provide better support at home to their children. One of the subtle benefits of portfolios that encourage self-assessment is that parents and children can communicate about ongoing schoolwork. Parents do not have to rely on periodic reports of test scores and grades to know how well their children are doing in school. More frequent information and better communication from schools may also build a supportive rather than evaluative role for parents. When all of the stakeholders are involved in children's education, there is more trust and shared goal setting. Parents and teachers understand each other's style of interaction and how they are trying to foster each child's development and education.

SUGGESTED READINGS

Anthony, R. J., Johnson, T. O., Mickelson, N. I., & Preece, A. (1991). *Evaluating literacy: A perspective for change.* Portsmouth, NH: Heinemann.

Graves, D. H., & Sunstein, B. S. (1992). *Portfolio portraits.* Portsmouth, NH: Heinemann.

Harp, B. (1991). *Assessment and evaluation in whole language classrooms.* Portsmouth, NH: Heinemann.

goal five

Becoming Reflective
Teachers

"There can be no significant innovation in education that does not have at its center the attitudes of teachers, and it is illusion to think otherwise." Postman and Weingartner, *Teaching as a Subversive Activity*

We have shown how teachers can encourage students to reflect on their own learning, to consider their strengths and weaknesses, to set purposes and goals for themselves, to provide help to others, and to feel pride in their accomplishments. Just as these self-reflections are important for learning, they are critical aspects of good teaching. Many of the teachers we observed examined their experiences with portfolios and reflected on their own professional development. To capture these insights about effective teaching, we interviewed several teachers who consistently modeled self-evaluation, persistence, revision, and optimism about progress in their own behavior as they worked with students.

CHARACTERISTICS OF REFLECTIVE TEACHERS

Reflective teachers engage in *self-evaluation* constantly, through both observation of student behavior and introspection into their own behavior. They are keen observers of students in their classrooms. Reflective teachers regularly set goals for themselves that they measure by the degree of understanding displayed by their students. Thus, they regard student responses and learning as daily assessments of teaching, considering them to be the definitive gauge of their success. In our interview with Lynn, a first-grade teacher, we glimpse this process of self-evaluation:

Interviewer: How do you go about evaluating your teaching? What is it that you think you do?

Lynn: I'm really conscious to think about it a lot. And I think every year— things that I'd like to do *better* the next year. And I'll look at things that I thought went really well that year. Like I said, I spend a lot of time reading a lot of literature in the field on my own because I just love reading about it so much. And I'm very hard on myself and I think, I don't measure up to all of these wonderful teachers that I read about sometimes. Sometimes I make lists, and I'll say,

"These are things I felt went particularly well with the students, these are things I think I need to change next year." And I'll make them goals for myself—real goals. [For example,] one of the goals I had *this* year that I felt went very well was ... to include more parents in my classroom and have better parent interaction so that they would understand some of the things that we are doing. And this year I ended up with some of these parents being some of my best friends, and *they* were all hugging and crying with me when the school year was over, wanting to know if *they* could come back and visit me ... I thought that was ... that's real important. I think it's very important because *I* consider myself a lifelong learner—that I'm always growing and learning, especially in my area that I've chosen to spend most of my life in. And so I'm constantly going to ... conferences, and reading, and trying to reevaluate and grow *myself*. And an important part of this— now, this may sound silly—but I purposely take classes. For example, I took a class in dance that was very hard for me with a teacher [who] has, nationwide, won competitions, because he's an excellent teacher. And I've sat and analyzed *his* teaching style and how he was teaching me, and [I put] myself back in the place of a learner, having to learn something that's very hard, difficult for me. And I feel that when you go back in a "learner" mode again, it reminds [you of] what it's like for those kids, to go back and learn how to be patient .... How is it that this teacher brings out such excellence in us? How can I bring out that excellence in my students? How can I make them all shine in the areas that they're good in?

In addition to observing the effects of their teaching, reflective teachers also engage in self-evaluation. Many teachers keep journals in which they make regular entries of a personal nature. Through journal writing, teachers pose questions to themselves that are not easily answered by the students or themselves, such as, "Am I providing enough individual attention to my students?" "How can I integrate the district requirements with the projects I enjoy, so that my excitement is conveyed to the students?" and "What can I do to make sure students see the connection between the reading they do in science and the problem solving they do in real life?" Teachers use journals to explore these and other issues in the same way they encourage their students to use journals. Journal writing then becomes a tool for teachers that they use to record and clarify thoughts. Many of the professional issues they examine are resolved by these reflections.

In addition to evaluating their own performance, reflective teachers are *persistent* in pursuing their goals. They regularly evaluate their progress toward achieving their goals. As teachers plan and adjust their approach to students, they keep their goals in mind and constantly strive toward them. This is illustrated by Ms. Collins, a fifth-grade teacher we interviewed, who had been successfully using portfolios in her classroom. Like most self-regulated teachers, Ms. Collins constantly sets new goals for herself and strives to attain them. This quality of persistence is apparent in these comments regarding portfolios:

> Interviewer: How has your understanding and use of portfolios changed throughout the year?
>
> Ms. Collins: It's changed only in that I feel I keep pushing the edge. I feel like there is more I can do with them. I feel they can serve my purposes better and that I have to facilitate a little bit better and try to gain the objectives that I want using them. In other words, teaching reading from them, teaching better story

structure … to really begin to apply those more and use the kids' writing more rather than just as a collection of their work, really use that to teach them and get them to improve their writing.

The modifications that Ms. Collins is willing to make in her classroom organization and in her lessons indicates the flexibility apparent in a self-reflective teacher. As she assesses the effectiveness of her use of portfolios, she identifies adjustments that she would like to make. Striving for improvement is not viewed by reflective teachers as failure. Rather, it is viewed as revision in a process. Self-reflective teachers *revise* their concepts as they make adjustments to new learning. They read professional journals, attend conferences, and participate in professional organizations, so that they are aware of changes occurring in the field. They appreciate the dynamic nature of learning in themselves as well as in their students; therefore, they expect to make frequent changes in their teaching practices.

Teachers use professional journals, conferences, and workshops to reflect on their own practices.

Another teacher we interviewed, Ms. Harrison, teaches fifth grade. She described her thoughts regarding portfolios and her desire to improve their effectiveness as an assessment tool:

Interviewer: How could you improve your ways of using portfolios?

Ms. Harrison: Next year, I really want to take a good look at how I'm doing the assessing. I started this year looking at scales to use for both reading and writing. I've got the information, but it was one of those things that had to take a back seat. So next year, I really want to work on … what are you looking for when you look at a piece of writing? And I have a lot of this information in my head, but how do I get it down, so I can comfortably record it? It's going to be very important for me next year.

Comments from a sixth-grade teacher, Mr. Wong, illustrate the process reflective teachers undergo as they consider certain aspects of their teaching. Decisions are not made quickly, but by observation and careful questioning, before conclusions are finally formed:

> Interviewer: How has your understanding and use of portfolios changed over the past year and up to now?
>
> Mr. Wong: I'm starting to see it as an assessment tool, rather than a program. When we started school ... the kids were picking their own work and getting to be self-reflective. And I liked the idea of them having a portfolio, and the kids were responding real well to the idea. I think for me, that I'm beginning to see the value of it as a major assessment. And maybe it's even serving to show the need to devalue our present system of assessment.

Although teachers frequently encounter problems that are not easily solved, such as where and to what extent portfolios fit into their classrooms, a sense of *optimism* pervades their work. When asked how she views herself in her profession, Carol illustrates the excitement that reflective teachers generate when they consider their past and future growth:

> Interviewer: Then generally, would you say that you're pleased with your progress as a teacher?
>
> Carol: Yes, but I'm also excited to see the next step and where I'm gonna end up at when I grow up! Because it's always changing, it's always learning, and I'm always excited to see where I've been and how I've gotten there. Because for me, it's important to see the *process*, not just the product .... [When these reforms started several years ago,] that's when I started getting involved. And it

made a difference. It just made a difference, and it was like, "Yes, these are things that I've always wanted to do. These are things I've known about literature and reading, but hadn't quite had the validity to back me up." And I feel it's given new life to my teaching, it makes me excited every year in August to want to go back again, and to be excited about the challenges that I'm going to encounter each year, because each year is a different year ... different kids, different parents. And you never know how it's going to turn out until June!

Like all good teachers, Carol sets high standards for herself. She feels responsible for the success of her students, and she regards her performance as key to their success. Even though reflective teachers are not easily satisfied, they are typically pleased with the progress they have made as teachers, and they expect to continue to grow in understanding as the years evolve. Great teachers model the excitement of curiosity and discovery because they approach their daily lives and their jobs with the same feelings they want to elicit from their students.

CONSEQUENCES OF BEING REFLECTIVE

Most of the teachers we interviewed were fortunate to work in schools that provided atmospheres conducive to self-reflection. The principals supported and encouraged teachers to try new things. The relationships between the principals we observed and their teachers were collegial in spite of their different roles. The teachers we spoke with were also fortunate to work with other teachers who enjoyed *collaborating* on projects throughout the year. Working with other teachers at the same grade level in planning curriculum activities encourages teachers to appreciate each others' special talents, to draw upon each other as resources, and to provide support for their own teaching. Janice explained how her relationship with other teachers at her grade level enhanced her teaching:

> Interviewer: Can you tell me how your relationships with other colleagues have changed?
>
> Janice: I kind of felt it was wonderful to have someone to fly ideas off of because otherwise you're hanging out there by yourself, not knowing is this right, is this wrong … and then you have parents questioning you, and this way, we're all kind of working, collaborating together.
>
> Interviewer: So did you do that regularly?
>
> Janice: Yes, we did. We had movies every other Friday and all … we would put four of our classes together, and while the kids were watching this movie for like, an hour, we would sit and discuss, "What are we gonna do?" But we all had individual teaching styles, so although we would decide on similar things to do and maybe like a culminating thing together, we all had our different ways of approaching things in the classroom.
>
> Interviewer: Sometimes it's really difficult to creatively come up with some times that teachers can share. That's probably one of the biggest problems that we have, is commonality together.
>
> Janice: I think so, too. And now at this school … we have tried to use our recess time, and we've also enjoyed working with just the three of us out of the five who have started working together, and we've had a couple of dinners together at school, like we'll order out pizza and stay after school ….

Interviewer: Oh, really? So you'll stay over ....

Janice: And we've done that once a month and come up with, like, a common calendar saying, you know, this is how we're gonna integrate our day—our science, and then math, and this is ... these are the different things we are doing ... and we'd always try to come up with ... about every other month, a big culminating center day, where we would have centers in all of our different rooms and parents that would come in. To go along with the themes and the science things that we were doing.

For many teachers, this represents a major change from the way they previously approached teaching. For example, Janice used to view her colleagues as people with whom she could share materials. and the relationship seldom progressed beyond that point. Now she considers them instrumental in her own development. She seeks their advice regarding students, and she values their opinions and insight concerning teaching in general. Teachers who engage in collegial relationships benefit by an increased sense of respect and support that they offer to each other. No longer engaged in a solitary effort, collegial teachers feel that the underlying philosophy of their teaching is strengthened by open discussions. They depend on each other as key influences in their personal and professional development.

Most districts have a written curriculum that they are committed to teach for the continuity and quality of education. Teachers in the district are typically required to deliver the prescribed curriculum using the materials provided for that purpose. In the framework of the curriculum, however, the teachers we interviewed were able to choose their methods of teaching as long as the results benefited student learning. The element of *choice* in determining the focus of their teaching is as important to teachers as it is for their students. When teachers choose their focus, they feel a greater commitment to ensure its success, as the following comments from Chris, an eighth-grade teacher, indicate:

> I think I try to make realistic goals for myself—ones that I'm interested in growing in my own areas for myself because then I think those are the ones, like, always ... when you're self-motivated and you're a self-learner, you *want* to accomplish those goals because no one's telling you that you *must* do these things. It's because you love it and you *want* to do it.

The ability to determine the focus of their teaching has an additional benefit for teachers, in that they are comfortable with the *challenge* it poses. They are aware of the strengths that will enable them to achieve the goals they set for themselves. They are also aware of areas in which they are not as strong, and they address them directly. Journals are helpful to teachers as they grapple with the challenge of their commitments. Through writing, teachers examine the areas they feel are weakest, and they set personal goals that will enable them to develop in those areas. It is not unusual for teachers to feel overwhelmed by the goals they have chosen to pursue. When asked how she knows she is attempting to do too much, Lynn offered a simple explanation:

> Lynn: How do I know when it's too much? I know if I feel stressed out and I'm passing that stress on to the kids. Then it's no longer enjoyable or fun .... Then I've got to pull back, because when *I'm* stressed, thinking I've got to get all of these things covered, then it's going to stress the kids out, and they're not going to ... get from it what they should.
>
> Interviewer: And they can sense that ...
>
> Lynn: They sense that ... they sense that with their teacher. Because I try not

to have that kind of environment. It needs to be relaxed enough that people *can* make mistakes, learn from them and move on. And if the kids are feeling, "we've gotta do this, this, this, and this, and we have two minutes to get it done," they're not gonna learn from that.

As Lynn's comments show, reflective teachers are cognizant of how they're feeling, and they try to look for clues from the kids. By consistently addressing issues and evaluating their progress relative to each goal, a sense of accomplishment is attained. Clearly, these teachers display the kind of self-reflective behavior that they are nurturing in their students. They also display characteristics of self-regulated learners. Reflective teachers have declarative knowledge of the field. That is, they possesses the content knowledge in reading, math, science, and social science as well as knowledge of pedagogy in each of those domains. They have procedural knowledge pertaining to pedagogy so that they can successfully implement the teaching strategies they have learned. Some of their procedural knowledge was learned in school; however, most of it is the result of experience and their own sensitivity to student responses. Reflective teachers understand that there are differences between individuals and groups of children, as well as differences in contexts of learning. Therefore, they adjust their approach to fit the situation. They apply their conditional knowledge consistently as they guide students toward understanding concepts and using the skills they learn in school. Finally, reflective teachers apply volitional strategies for maintaining a focus toward their chosen goals. They are persistent, strategic, and directed in their efforts to provide the best possible learning environment for their students.

The teachers we interviewed identified many areas of change that have occurred as they have moved to a more student-centered approach to teaching. All agreed that students are no longer spectators in the classroom, but rather crucial participants who are responsible for their roles in each learning situation. Because students actively demonstrate their understanding of key concepts in a variety of ways throughout the day, teachers' views of assessment have altered considerably as well. Although most students were once assessed at the end of a unit of study, often with paper-and-pencil tasks, teachers now see many viable alternatives to multiple-choice tests. Teachers consider the activities they plan for their students to promote learning as well as to provide daily opportunities for assessment in the students' regular environment. As their ideas about teaching changed, a more functional, performance-based view of assessment emerged.

> Teachers changed their ideas about assessment and learner-centered teaching after observing the impact of portfolios.

Perhaps the biggest change identified in our interviews with teachers has to do with the concept of themselves as teachers. Covering a certain amount of material during the year used to be the prevailing goal for most. However, teachers now view their charge in a much larger context:

> Interviewer: How about the way that you *view* teaching ... have the changes you've made had an effect on that?
>
> Donna: Yes. I think it's made teaching more fun, more enjoyable, more exciting, more interactive ... all the things I hope my students feel. I feel it's changed teaching. I think before, I felt we had to cover these curriculum areas in this order, in this sequence, to be a good teacher. And I found out, well, no, it doesn't quite work that way. That you have to yes, cover the curriculum and nudge your students along, but you can also watch the kids and pounce upon those wonderful moments that they show you, and integrate it all. Cover the curriculum, be a good kid-watcher, and have them excited and learning, too.

Donna thinks of teaching as more of a calling, rather than a job. Her calling is to model the behaviors of a lifelong learner so that her students will adopt those same attitudes for themselves. We are constantly reminded by the insights of teachers that we are all lifelong learners and that understanding ourselves and the things that promote our own motivated acquisition of knowledge provides valuable guidelines for helping children discover the same processes in themselves.

1

Reflecting: Consider the characteristics of intrinsic motivation that we discussed for students and apply them to teachers. For each statement below, mark an X on the line to indicate whether you agree or disagree with the statement. Higher levels of agreement indicate that you probably have high intrinsic motivation for teaching in your school.

1. I make many choices about instruction and assessment activities in my classroom.

Strongly Disagree   Disagree   Neutral   Agree   Strongly Agree

2. I adjust my teaching schedule and practices so that new things are challenging not frustrating.

Strongly Disagree   Disagree   Neutral   Agree   Strongly Agree

3. I have a great deal of control over the pace, sequence, and integration of my instruction.

Strongly Disagree   Disagree   Neutral   Agree   Strongly Agree

4. Other teachers and staff in my school collaborate regularly to plan instruction and assessment.

Strongly Disagree   Disagree   Neutral   Agree   Strongly Agree

5. Professional development activities allow me to construct meaningful activities that fit my school.

Strongly Disagree   Disagree   Neutral   Agree   Strongly Agree

6. I work hard for my students and school because I know my efforts are appreciated and I feel proud of the accomplishments we have made together.

Strongly Disagree   Disagree   Neutral   Agree   Strongly Agree

2 **Responding:** Write yourself a letter about how your teaching has changed and what you plan to do differently this year. Describe how you would like students to react to your teaching. Then seal the letter and tape it to your calendar 3 to 4 months from now so you can read it when you are in a different frame of mind.

3 **Sharing:** Make a list of the six Cs that promote learning and motivation in schools—Choice, Challenge, Control, Collaboration, Constructing Meaning, and Consequences—like in the chart below, and post it on a wall in the teachers' lounge for teachers to write comments.

Students' Motivation	Good Examples I've Seen in Classrooms
Choice	
Challenge	
Control	
Collaboration	
Constructing Meaning	
Consequences	

4 **Reviewing:** Teachers, like students, need opportunities to reflect on their own performance and accomplishments. They need the feelings of satisfaction and confidence that follow completion of difficult tasks; they need to feel control and support for their efforts in order to sustain their motivation. We believe that teachers can benefit from reflecting, responding, and sharing new ideas just like students, and we hope that this book has stimulated you to consider learning, instruction, and assessment from a new perspective.

SUGGESTED READINGS

Herman, J. L., Aschbacher, P. R., & Winters, L. (1992). *A practical guide to alternative assessment.* Alexandria, VA: Association for Supervison and Curriculum Development.

Kemp, M. (1990). *Watching children read and write.* Portsmouth, NH: Heinemann.

Wolf, K. P. (1993). From informal to informed assessment: Recognizing the role of the classroom teacher. *Journal of Reading, 36,* 518–523.

final review

Learning, Developing,
and Becoming

"If you want to predict the future, invent it." John Scully

THE IMPORTANCE OF REFLECTION

Our own development as teachers during the last 20 years provides the foundation for the three major themes we have emphasized in this book. The first theme is the pervasive nature of reflection because it influences all of the participants in education. Reflection on classroom practices helps all stakeholders review, question, discuss, and understand how learning, instruction, curriculum, and assessment are interwoven and reciprocal. Our insights into changes in our own teaching and learning persuades us that reflection is a powerful process for promoting self-regulated learning—at all ages. We tried to capture these reflections in the comments of teachers, the letters from parents, and the samples of work by students, so that others can hear their voices. They are strong voices that show how people seek understanding and control in their daily lives and how proud they feel when reviewing children's accomplishments. Many psychological forces are evident in their reflections, including aspects of self-evaluation, effort and persistence, revision of plans and goals, and optimism about personal progress and future development. These processes are manifested in self-appraisal and self-management of one's own behavior and lead to positive self-regard.

> Reflection helps parents, teachers, and students understand the dynamics of learning, instruction, curriculum, and assessment.

Reflection operates in similar ways for all stakeholders. A review of past performance is motivated either internally or by someone else in order to examine the adequacy of one's performance. There may be additional motives provided by a desire for intrinsic mastery, by promises of extrinsic rewards, by threats of punishment, or by social collaboration. Regardless of the stimulus for personal reviews, all require a standard in order to judge one's progress. These standards for comparison are generally prior performance of the individual, external standards, or the performance of a peer or peer group. The resulting comparison leads to inferences about change, growth, and competence. For example, students might see improvement in their reading skills, parents might note children's developmental achievements, and teachers might evaluate children's performance relative to other students in the school. These interpretations about *levels* of performance also engender inferences about the *reasons* for performance. Thus, each stakeholder may construct plausible reasons for the observed performance, such as high effort or ability, effective strategies, or tutorial assistance. These reasons give rise to various emotional responses such as pride, guilt, satisfaction, or anger, depending on the attributions that are made (Weiner, 1992).

Both the processes and the outcomes of reflection are similar for children, teachers, and parents. The dynamics also apply to various lengths of time. Some reflections may be highly specific to a situation; they may focus on immediate performance and be embedded in tasks such as writing a letter. Other reflections address growth over time and may span days or years and be based on analysis of numerous work samples. Adults have more experiences to examine than do children, which allows us to see historical and developmental changes in ourselves in more detail, in more settings, and over distinct periods of time. Despite not having the obvious advantage of longevity, children can clearly gain insight into their own learning when given opportunities and encouragement.

ONGOING OPPORTUNITIES FOR REFLECTION

The second theme of this book addresses the importance of providing regular opportunities for reflection that are planned and embedded in everyday instruction and assessment activities. Teachers and children alike can become detached and disengaged from their learning if they are not provided frequent opportunities to reflect on their jobs and discuss their crafts of teaching and learning. Children from first grade on need to review their work at least once every week so that they internalize the standards and processes that teachers advocate and model.

> Students should have opportunities for reflection in daily instruction and assessment activities.

Students should review their performance and progress periodically during the year with parents and teachers so that there is shared understanding about the strengths, weaknesses, and goals for the students' learning. Similarly, teachers need opportunities to review their own teaching in nonevaluative and nonthreatening ways, not simply an annual conference with a principal. For example, teams of teachers may meet to discuss new aspects of their curricula or alternative assessments or ways to facilitate home–school communication as means to share their insights about what works in their classrooms. Most Asian schools provide teachers with several hours each day to work together, to observe each other, and to plan their classroom lessons together to stimulate reflection and help them to try new techniques (Stevenson & Stigler, 1992). Parents and administrators can benefit from opportunities to assess their roles as well. In the context of children's learning, the activities might be most valuable when they include the students so that their voices are heard directly. That is why we consider student-led conferences to be so valuable.

We have other suggestions for parents and administrators so that they can become more actively involved in child-centered classrooms. First, administrators or Parent–Teacher Association groups can conduct annual surveys, formal or informal, of their assessment policies and practices. This is necessary because most parents receive little information about assessment from school districts and often do not understand achievement test results (Barber, Paris, Evans, & Gadsden, 1992). Concerted efforts are needed to inform the public about the educational goals, curricula, and assessment practices in schools so that they do not depend on hearsay or media reports. Second, administrators can append self-assessment items to annual achievement tests given to students so that they can be assured that students gave their genuine efforts on the tests. Third, administrators can educate local media on proper and improper use of test data. Incidentally, we believe that the misuses of testing data in newspapers so routinely observed across the country can be changed significantly if districts would not test every pupil in all schools. Random sampling of students would prevent school-by-school and district-by-district comparisons while simultaneously saving a great deal of district money and student time. Fourth, parents and administrators can reevaluate the functions and adequacy of report cards to reflect changing notions of the curriculum and assessment (Afflerbach, 1993). These suggestions are intended to involve administrators and parents directly in the design and use of assessment data so that teachers and students are served better by new approaches to

> Self-assessment activities for students of all ages, kindergarten through university level, can be part of daily instruction and assessment.

assessment. Without the interactive participation of stakeholders at all levels, the process is at risk of being designed without a learner-centered focus.

Because self-assessment was ignored in traditional approaches to curriculum, instruction, and assessment, it is not common for teachers to include activities for reflection in their classrooms. When classroom procedures are driven by materials, textbooks, the district curriculum objectives or outcomes, and traditional achievement testing, teachers do not often include performance-based assessments or portfolios that can promote self-assessment. In these classrooms, students' production of "work" supersedes students' development of self-regulated learning. Parents are seldom involved in classrooms like these or in reviews of student performance beyond the annual parent–teacher conference and periodic report card. Whether intentional or not, these practices distance parents from the learning environments of their children. Teachers can lose a powerful influence and teaching ally when parents do not understand teachers' methods and goals and do not feel welcome in the classroom. Reflective assessments help to build a more interactive relationship among teachers, parents, and students.

We believe that self-assessment can be incorporated into every classroom in the United States from elementary grades through university-level training. The main obstacles are (a) the lack of knowledge about the importance of self-assessment for lifelong learning and (b) the lack of information about appropriate activities that promote self-assessment. We hope that readers will now understand how important self-assessment is to learners of all ages. We hope that they will begin to incorporate in their classrooms a variety of tasks that invite and foster self-assessment. These are intrinsically motivating activities that hold choices and challenges, that allow people to take control and feel a sense of efficacy, and that promote creativity and collaboration through help giving and help seeking. Activities that embody these characteristics stimulate children, teachers, and parents to become actively involved in assessing their roles in children's learning. Most of our suggestions and examples are interactive because we believe that the understanding of all stakeholders is enhanced when they review and discuss children's performance with someone else.

Finally, it is worth mentioning again that self-assessment is both a high-stakes and low-cost form of alternative assessment. Teachers do not have to sacrifice time from their curricula, purchase new materials, or give up the things that work in their classrooms. Activities that promote self-assessment can be part of the regular curriculum; indeed, they *should* be embedded in daily learning and assessment tasks such as journal writing, goal setting, and peer conferences. Recent trends to afford teachers more responsibility over assessment practices may present unforeseen problems if training in alternative assessment methods is not also included. Teachers must rise to this challenge and seize this opportunity for empowerment and control, or they may find reformers shifting their calls to nationalized testing as a more efficient solution. We urge teachers to incorporate assessment practices that allow students to review their own work and development for authentic purposes.

> Self-assessment is both a high-stakes and low-cost form of alternative assessment.

SELF-ASSESSMENT PROMOTES PERSONAL DEVELOPMENT

A third theme of this book is Development with a capital D because self-assessment is so fundamental to personal growth. Through reflection we evaluate our knowledge and skills, we improve them to meet higher standards, and we take pride in our accomplishments. Self-assessment of one's accomplishments and talents fosters these positive developmental outcomes. In this book, our examples were drawn from children in grades K–8 who are becoming lifelong students, but the developmental theme also applies to older students as well as teachers and parents. High school and college students, especially those who have had limited opportunities to reflect on their own learning, relish the chances to examine their strengths, styles, and weaknesses. Sometimes they are amazed by other people's reactions to their self-assessments, because they are so discordant with their own appraisals. What one student considers a liability is often unnoticed by a peer, and what a teacher or parent might most admire in a high school student may be overlooked by the adolescent entirely. Without opportunities to review and discuss their own learning, many students with 12 or more years of education remain naive or confused about their own abilities and accomplishments. Their development is thwarted if their estimates are unrealistically high or low, problems that may be as frequent among high achievers as low achievers.

Self-assessment is a basic part of students' thinking and motivation, crucial for continued development. In this sense, reflections are embedded in personal transformations because they are precursors to and consequences of change. The process of moving beyond old habits and seeing things from new perspectives can be characterized in several ways. From a cognitive point of view, it is equilibration or balancing new information with prior knowledge, according to Piaget. From a humanistic perspective, self-assessment is part of the process of "becoming," for example, transforming one's attitudes and beliefs into new views. We believe that students who use self-assessment to acquire greater insights into themselves and their education form more coherent theories about themselves and become more able students (Paris & Byrnes, 1989).

In the same vein, teachers who are reflective and who act to improve their teaching on the basis of their insights become master teachers who mentor and lead others. The act of becoming insightful helps teachers become more mindful of the way they challenge students and arrange their instructional environments. They become less defensive with parents as they become more aware of the competing forces and philosophies in their schools. They become more confident and satisfied. They become more articulate about their craft and they share their observations of teaching and learning. The interviews with teachers and our own personal reflections are testimonials to the power of self-assessment.

CONCLUSION

In closing, it is worth sharing two comments from colleagues on earlier drafts of this book in anticipation of similar reactions from other readers. The first comment we heard was, "I see this dark dragon lurking in the background that will doom all these ideas to failure. How do you make sure that the good things a child experiences in one classroom are there next year in a different classroom? What if the third grade teacher has a classroom like Joanie's but the fourth grade teacher is like Sister Mary Catherine who nearly killed me with her ruler? How can you make these things happen throughout the school? How can you have a system that has continuity if every teacher does her own thing?"

> Teachers who are reflective and who act to improve their teaching based on their insights become master teachers who mentor and lead others.

The key to continuity for students and parents is consensus within a school and district. This does not mean that all teachers have to use portfolios, journals, or letters to parents. Instead, consensus can be built from administrative policies that stipulate that all teachers will gather performance-based indicators of student achievement. These policies should be consistent with the district's outcomes or goals, evident in the report cards and other assessment practices, and supported by professional development activities for teachers and community information for the public. The policies should allow school principals and staffs, as well as individual teachers, to make choices about the kinds of evidence that they collect from students.

The key to continuity in schools is staff development that has high expectations, collegial support, professional recognition by the community, and adequate resources to reach the goals. Consensus can be established within schools when the staff shares the same vision for assessment, when they share the same terms and concepts, and when they agree to collect similar evidence. For example, K–3 teachers might agree to collect miscue analyses from every student once a year, teachers in grades 4–8 might collect samples of students' writing in three different genres, the entire staff might decide to give students an attitude survey at the beginning of the year. Consensus building requires sharing and negotiating, which lead to teamwork. This is a wonderful by-product of a staff project aimed at creating assessments to promote self-regulated learning.

The second comment we heard was, "OK, where is this school? Mars? Because it doesn't sound like any school I've been in and I want to move there. I want to teach in one of those schools and I want my kids to go there too." Have we painted an idealistic picture? Of course. Have we established unattainable goals? Definitely not. All of the quotes and examples are real people sharing their feelings about life in their schools, but together the sum is greater than any individual child, teacher, or parent. We did not include the humdrum activities, the boring quotations, or the embarrassing work samples—but they were evident in every classroom we visited. Are we hiding "reality"? No, we chose not to convey mundane reflections but rather showcase the thoughtful comments that stand as evidence of the insights that are possible. Just as pearls are not found in every oyster, insight is not found in every self-assessment. Although each person participated in self-assessment and benefited from the reviews and discussions, each individual did so uniquely. However, at every grade in many different schools, teachers told us that some students startled them with their insights, their efforts, and their excitement about reviewing and discussing their work.

We are excited to share these ideas with you because we have seen the positive and profound impact that new kinds of assessment can have on students, teachers, and parents. Their reflections and deep engagement that emanates from new insights provides motivation for us all to try new approaches to teaching and learning—to move away from the shackles of tradition and habit that we endure in the classroom because we are unsure of the risks and liabilities of portfolios and performance assessments. Teachers, like students everywhere, need to loosen their imaginations and create classrooms that excite curiosity and inquiry and invite self-assessment. We have been inspired by the differences that teachers have made in their schools and in the lives of their students, and we hope that their stories and voices in this book inspire others to design and use new assessments that are child-centered, authentic, and empowering.

appendix

Learner-Centered
Psychological Principles

The following pages are excerpted from "Learner-centered psychological principles: Guidelines for school redesign and reform" (pp. 6-9). Produced by the Presidential Task Force on Psychology in Education, American Psychological Association, Washington, DC, January 1993.

The following 12 psychological principles pertain to the *learner* and the *learning process*. They focus on psychological factors that are primarily internal to the learner while recognizing external environmental or contextual factors that interact with these internal factors. These principles also attempt to deal holistically with learners in the context of real-world learning situations. Thus, they must be understood as an organized set of principles and not be treated in isolation. The principles refer to metacognitive, cognitive, affective, developmental, and social factors that influence students' academic success. The principles apply to all learners, regardless of age.

METACOGNITIVE AND COGNITIVE FACTORS

Principle 1: The Nature of the Learning Process

Learning is a natural process of pursuing personally meaningful goals, and it is active, volitional, and internally mediated; it is a process of discovering and constructing meaning from information and experience, filtered through the learner's unique perceptions, thoughts and feelings.

Students have a natural inclination to learn and pursue personally relevant learning goals. They are capable of assuming personal responsibility for learning—monitoring, checking for understanding, and becoming active, self-directed learners—in an environment that takes past learning into account, ties new learning to personal goals, and actively engages students in their own learning process. In meaningful life situations, even very young children naturally engage in self-directed learning activities to pursue personal goals. During the learning process, individuals create their own meanings and interpretations on the basis of previously existing understandings and beliefs.

Principle 2: Goals of the Learning Process

The learner seeks to create meaningful, coherent representations of knowledge regardless of the quantity and quality of data available.

Learners generate integrated, commonsense representations and explanations for even poorly understood or communicated facts, concepts, principles, or theories. Learning processes operate holistically in the sense that internally consistent understandings emerge that may or may not be valid from an objective, externally oriented perspective. As learners internalize values and meanings within a discipline, however, they can refine their conceptions by filling in gaps, resolving inconsistencies, and revising prior conceptions.

Principle 3: The Construction of Knowledge

The learner links new information with existing and future-oriented knowledge in uniquely meaningful ways.

Given that backgrounds and experiences of individuals can differ dramatically, and given that the mind works to link information meaningfully and holistically, learners organize information in ways that are uniquely meaningful to them. A goal in formal education is to have all learners create shared understandings and conceptions regarding fundamental knowledge and skills that define and lead to valued learning outcomes. In these situations, teachers can assist learners in acquiring and integrating knowledge (e.g., by teaching them strategies for constructing meaning, organizing content, accessing prior knowledge, relating new knowledge to general themes or principles, storing or practicing what they have learned, visualizing future uses for the knowledge).

Principle 4: Higher-order thinking

Higher-order strategies for "thinking about thinking"—for overseeing and monitoring mental operations—facilitate creative and critical thinking and the development of expertise.

During early to middle childhood, learners become capable of a metacognitive or executive level of thinking about their own thinking that includes self-awareness, self-inquiry or dialogue, self-monitoring, and self-regulation of the processes and contents of thoughts, knowledge structures, and memories. Learners' awareness of their personal agency or control over thinking and learning processes promotes higher levels of commitment, persistence, and involvement in learning. To foster this self-awareness of agency, learners need settings where their personal interests, values, and goals are respected and accommodated.

AFFECTIVE FACTORS

Principle 5: Motivational Influences on Learning

The depth and breadth of information processed, and what and how much is learned and remembered, are influenced by (a) self-awareness and beliefs about personal control, competence and ability; (b) clarity and saliency of personal values, interests, and goals; (c) personal expectations for success or failure; (d) affect, emotion, and general states of mind; and (e) the resulting motivation to learn.

The rich internal world of beliefs, goals, expectations, and feelings can enhance or interfere with learners' quality of thinking and information processing. The relationship among thoughts, mood, and behavior underlies individuals' psychological health and ability to learn. Learners' interpretations or cognitive constructions of reality can impede positive motivation, learning, and performance, as can negative thoughts and feelings.

Conversely, positive learning experiences can help reverse negative thoughts and feelings and enhance student motivation to learn.

Principle 6: Intrinsic Motivation to Learn

Individuals are naturally curious and enjoy learning, but intense negative cognitions and emotions (e.g., feeling insecure, worrying about failure, being self-conscious or shy, and fearing corporal punishment, ridicule, or stigmatization labels) thwart this enthusiasm.

Educators must support and develop students' natural curiosity or intrinsic motivation to learn, rather than "fixing them" or driving them by fear of corporal punishment or excessive punishments of any kind. Also, both positive interpersonal support and instruction in self-control strategies can offset factors that interfere with optimal learning—factors such as low self-awareness; negative beliefs; lack of learning goals; negative expectations for success; and anxiety, insecurity, or pressure.

Principle 7: Characteristics of Motivation-Enhancing Learning Tasks

Curiosity, creativity and higher-order thinking are simulated by relevant, authentic learning tasks of optimal difficulty and novelty for each student.

Positive affect, creativity, and flexible and insightful thinking are promoted in contexts that learners perceive as personally relevant and meaningful. For example, students need opportunities to make choices in line with their interests and to have the freedom to change the course of learning in light of self-awareness, discovery or insights. Projects that are comparable to real-world situations in complexity and duration elicit students' higher-order thinking skills and creativity. In, addition, curiosity is enhanced when students can work on personally relevant learning tasks of optimal difficulty and novelty.

DEVELOPMENTAL FACTORS

Principle 8: Developmental Constraints and Opportunities

Individuals progress through stages of physical, intellectual, emotional, and social development that are a function of unique genetic and environmental factors.

Children learn best when material is appropriate to their developmental level and is presented in an enjoyable and interesting way, while challenging their intellectual, emotional, physical, and social development. Unique environmental factors (e.g., the quality of language interactions between adult and child and parental involvement in the child's schooling) can influence development in each area. An overemphasis on developmental readiness, however, may preclude learners from demonstrating that they are more capable intellectually than schools, teachers, or parents allow them to show. Awareness and understanding of developmental differences of children with special emotional, physical or intellectual disabilities as well as special abilities can greatly facilitate efforts to create optimal contexts for learning.

PERSONAL AND SOCIAL FACTORS

Principle 9: Social and Cultural Diversity

Learning is facilitated by social interactions and communications with others in flexible, diverse (in age, culture, family background, etc.), and adaptive instructional settings.

Learning is facilitated when the learner has an opportunity to interact with various students representing different cultural and family backgrounds, interests, and values. Learning settings that allow for and respect diversity encourage flexible thinking as well as social competence and moral development. In such settings, individuals have an opportunity for perspective taking and reflective thinking, thereby leading to insights and breakthroughs to new knowledge.

Principle 10: Social Acceptance, Self-Esteem, and Learning

Learning and self-esteem are heightened when individuals are in respectful and caring relationships with others who see their potential, genuinely appreciate their unique talents, and accept them as individuals.

Quality personal relationships give the individual access to higher-order, healthier levels of thinking, feeling and behaving. Teachers' (or significant adults') states of mind, stability, trust, and caring are preconditions for establishing a sense of belonging, self-respect, self-acceptance, and positive climate for learning. Healthier levels of thinking are those that are less self-conscious, insecure, irrational, and self-depreciating. Self-esteem and learning are mutually reinforcing.

INDIVIDUAL DIFFERENCES

Principle 11: Individual Differences in Learning

Although basic principles of learning, motivation, and effective instruction apply to all learners (regardless of ethnicity, race, gender, physical ability, religion, or socioeconomic status), learners have different capabilities and preferences for learning mode and strategies. These differences are a function of environment (what is learned and communicated in different cultures or other social groups) and heredity (what occurs naturally as a function of genes).

The same basic principles of learning, motivation, and effective instruction apply to all learners. However, individuals are born with and develop unique capabilities and talents and have acquired through learning and social acculturation different preferences for how they like to learn and the pace at which they learn. Also, student differences and curricular and environmental conditions are key factors that greatly affect learning outcomes. Understanding and valuing cultural differences and the cultural contexts in which learners develop enhances the possibilities for designing and implementing learning environments that are optimal for all students.

Principle 12: Cognitive Filters

Personal beliefs, thoughts, and understandings resulting from prior learning and interpretations become the individual's basis for constructing reality and interpreting life experiences.

Unique cognitive constructions form a basis for beliefs and attitudes about others. Individuals then operate out of these "separate realities" as if they were true for everyone, often leading to misunderstandings and conflict. Awareness and understanding of these phenomena allow greater choice in what one believes and more control over the degree to which one's beliefs influence one's actions and enable one to see and take into account others' points of view. The cognitive, emotional, and social development of a child and the way that child interprets life experiences are a product of prior schooling, home, culture, and community factors.

glossary

authentic assessment—Multiple ways of evaluating students' learning, achievements, motivation, and attitudes that are consistent with classroom goals, curricula, and instructional methods.

author's chair—A method of allowing children to read or tell their stories to others, usually in special times and places, so that they assume the role of authors.

book log—A record that lists the books that children have read, often including brief comments or parents' initials to signify that the books have been read at home.

conditional knowledge—An aspect of metacognition that informs people about the appropriate conditions and situations in which knowledge and skills should be applied, e.g., when, where, and why to apply their strategies.

constructing meaning—The actions of creating meaningful sequences, episodes, and narrative accounts of meaning during reading, writing, and storytelling.

declarative knowledge—The knowledge about what strategies and skills are available or appropriate for solving a problem.

dialogue journal—A notebook or journal that records a conversation or dialogue, typically between a teacher and a student about events in school, on a periodic basis.

expository text—Text that conveys information and facts, such as the text commonly found in newspapers and science books.

extrinsic motivation—Sources of motivation that are outside of the person, such as money, rewards, and praise provided by other people.

flexible groups—Instructional organization of students into various groups on the basis of such factors as interests, abilities, random assignment, and friendships so that grouping does not reflect a single dimension, such as ability, in a classroom.

focused assessment—An assessment of students' performance that is limited in time and scope to evaluate a specific accomplishment.

formative assessment—Diagnostic evaluation that helps to design and guide instruction.

home portfolios—A system of collecting samples of schoolwork and accomplishments so that they can be shared with families and saved for the future.

integrated language arts—Instructional activities that integrate listening, speaking, reading, writing, and viewing across the curriculum.

intrinsic motivation—Goals and rewards for learning are provided by personal needs, interests, and expertise rather than external rewards.

learner-centered—Practices in schools that are sensitive to the individual and developmental characteristics of each student.

metacognition—"Thinking about thinking," or knowledge related to self-appraisal and self-regulation of one's thinking and actions.

narrative text—Text that is written in a story genre with a setting, characters, and plot; it may be fiction or nonfiction.

ongoing assessment—Repeated evaluations over time of the same skills, concepts, or attitudes to examine longitudinal learning and other changes.

performance assessment—Evaluations that are based on observations of the behavior of a person performing a complex task such as reading a text, writing a report, or solving a problem.

portfolios—A systematic way of collecting and reviewing samples of work that illustrate personal accomplishments, processes, and styles.

procedural knowledge—The knowledge about how to apply skills and how various strategies and problem-solving tactics operate.

response journal—A collected set of reactions, usually to texts that one has read or written.

rubric—A set of descriptions of various explicit levels that specify different standards or levels of performance on a task.

self-assessment—Reflections and insights about one's own accomplishments, progress, and development.

self-efficacy—The perceptions and feelings that one is capable and competent to effect a particular outcome and that one ought to act accordingly.

self-regulated learning—The direction and control of one's actions, thinking, and emotions to pursue and attain particular goals.

standardized tests—Criterion-referenced and norm-referenced tests of ability and achievement given in a uniform manner to assess performance relative to specific criteria or compared to other people.

strategic reading—The selection, use, and management of specific strategies (such as skimming, rereading, and summarizing) to enhance comprehension, memory, and enjoyment of text.

summative assessments—Evaluations that provide scores or reports of completed assignments used to measure progress and compare relative performance levels.

TE—Teachers' edition of instructional materials that provides lesson plans and suggestions.

test pollution—The variability created among tests by the use of a wide range of ethical and unethical practices that threaten the validity of the scores.

thinking logs—Records of problem solving used to document students' thinking about assignments and problems.

volitional strategies—Tactics that people use to stay committed to their goals and to prevent distractions from changing their efforts or persistence.

whole language—A philosophy of literacy instruction based on the integration of cognitive, affective, and motivational characteristics of children and applied to literacy learning with meaningful materials.

references

Afflerbach, P. (1993). Report cards and reading. *The Reading Teacher*, *46*, 458–465.

Ames, C., & Archer, J. (1988). Achievement goals in the classroom: Students' learning strategies and motivation processes. *Journal of Educational Psychology*, *80*, 260–267.

Au, K. H., Scheu, J. A., Kawakami, A. J., & Herman, P. A. (1990). Assessment and accountability in a whole language curriculum. *The Reading Teacher, 43*, 574–578.

Barber, B. L., Paris, S. G., Evans, M., & Gadsden, V. (1992). Policies for reporting test results to parents. *Educational Measurement: Issues and Practices, 11*, 15–20.

Brown, A., Bransford, J., Ferrara, R., & Campione, J. (1983). Learning, remembering, and understanding. In J. H. Flavell & E. M. Markman (Eds.), *Carmichael's manual of child psychology* (Vol. 1, pp. 77–106). New York: Wiley.

Bruner, J. (1961). *The process of education.* Cambridge, MA: Harvard University Press.

Calfee, R., & Hiebert, E. (1990). Classroom assessment of reading. In R. Barr, M. Kamil, P. Mosenthal, & P. D. Pearson (Eds.), *Handbook of reading research* (2nd ed., pp. 281–309). New York: Longman.

Calkins, L. (1986). *The art of teaching writing.* Portsmouth, NH: Heinemann.

Clifford, M. (1991). Risk taking: Theoretical, empirical, and educational considerations. *Educational Psychologist, 26,* 263–297.

Corno, L. (1992). Encouraging students to take responsibility for learning and performance. *Elementary School Journal, 93,* 69–83.

Covington, M. C. (1992). *Making the grade.* Cambridge, England: Cambridge University Press.

De Charms, R. (1968). *Personal causation: The internal affective determinants of behavior.* New York: Academic Press.

Deci, E. L., Vallerand, R. J., Pelletier, L. G., & Ryan, R. M. (1991). Motivation and education: The self-determination perspective. *Educational Psychologist, 26,* 325–346.

Dweck, C., & Leggett, E. (1988). A social–cognitive approach to motivation and personality. *Psychological Review, 95,* 256–273.

Glazer, S. M., & Brown, C. S. (1993). *Portfolios and beyond: Collaborative assessment in reading and writing.* Norwood, MA: Christopher-Gordon.

Graves, D. (1983). *Writing: Teachers and children at work.* Portsmouth, NH: Heinemann.

Graves, D., & Sunstein, B. S. (1992). *Portfolio portraits.* Portsmouth, NH: Heinemann.

Haladyna, T., Nolen, S. B., & Haas, N. S. (1991). Raising standardized achievement test scores and the origins of test score pollution. *Educational Researcher, 20,* 2–7.

Herman, J. L., Aschbacher, P. R., & Winters, L. (1992). *A practical guide to alternative assessment.* Alexandria, VA: Association for Supervision and Curriculum Development.

Lave, J., & Wegner, E. (1991). *Situated learning: Legitimate peripheral participation.* Cambridge, MA: Cambridge University Press.

Linn, R. L., Baker, E. L., & Dunbar, S. B. (1991). Complex, performance-based assessment: Expectations and validation criteria. *Educational Researcher, 20,* 15–21.

Madaus, G. F., & Tan, A. G. A. (1993). The growth of assessment. In G. Cawelti (Ed.), *Challenges and achievements of American education* (pp. 53–79). Alexandria, VA: Association for Supervision and Curriculum Development.

McCombs, B. L., & Marzano, R. J. (1990). Putting the self in self-regulated learning: The self as agent in integrating skill and will. *Educational Psychologist, 25,* 51–69.

Meece, J. L., Blumenfeld, P. C., & Puro, P. (1989). A motivational analysis of elementary science learning environments. In M. Matyas, K. Tobin, & B. Fraser (Eds.), *Looking into windows: Qualitative research in science education* (pp. 13–23). Washington, DC: American Association for the Advancement of Science.

Messick, S. (1989). Validity. In R. Linn (Ed.), *Educational measurement* (3rd ed., pp. 13–104). New York: Macmillan.

Newman, R. S., & Goldin, L. (1990). Children's reluctance to seek help with schoolwork. *Journal of Educational Psychology, 82,* 92–100.

Palincsar, A. S., & Brown, A. (1984). Reciprocal teaching of comprehension-fostering and comprehension-monitoring activities. *Cognition and Instruction, 1,* 117–175.

Paris, S. G. (1994). The dark side of standardized testing and the promise of portfolios. *The Kamehameha Journal of Education,* 1–15.

Paris, S. G., & Byrnes, J. P. (1989). The constructivist approach to self-regulation and learning in the classroom. In B. Zimmerman & D. Schunk (Eds.), *Self-regulated learning and academic achievement: Theory, research, and practice* (pp. 169–200). New York: Springer-Verlag.

Paris, S. G., Calfee, R. C., Filby, N., Hiebert, E., Pearson, P. D., Valencia, S. W., & Wolf, K. P. (1992). A framework for authentic literacy assessment. *The Reading Teacher, 46,* 88–98.

Paris, S. G., & Cross, D. R. (1983). Ordinary learning: Pragmatic connections among children's beliefs, motives, and actions. In J. Bisanz, G. Bisanz, & R. Kail (Eds.), *Learning in children* (pp. 137–169). New York: Springer-Verlag.

Paris, S. G., Lawton, T. A., & Turner, J. C. (1992). Reforming achievement testing to promote students' learning. In C. Collins & J. Mangieri (Eds.), *Teaching thinking: An agenda for the twenty-first century* (pp. 223–241). Hillsdale, NJ: Erlbaum.

Paris, S. G., Lawton, T. A., Turner, J. C., & Roth, J. L. (1991). A developmental perspective on standardized achievement testing. *Educational Researcher, 20,* 12–20.

Paris, S. G., Lipson, M. Y., & Wixson, K. (1983). Becoming a strategic reader. *Contemporary Educational Psychology, 8,* 293–316.

Paris, S. G., & Turner, J. T. (1994). Situated motivation. In P. Pintrich, C. Weinstein, & D. Brown (Eds.), *Student motivation, cognition, and learning: Essays in honor of Wilbert J. McKeachie.* Hillsdale, NJ: Erlbaum.

Paris, S. G., & Winograd, P. W. (1990). How metacognition can promote academic learning and instruction. In B. J. Jones & L. Idol (Eds.), *Dimensions of thinking and cognitive instruction* (pp. 15–51). Hillsdale, NJ: Erlbaum.

Raphael, T. E., & Englert, C. S. (1990). Writing and reading: Partners in constructing meaning. *The Reading Teacher, 43,* 388–400.

Resnick, L., & Resnick, D. (1990). Tests as standards of achievement in school. In *The uses of standardized tests in American education* (pp. 63–80). Princeton, NJ: Educational Testing Service.

Rogoff, B. (1990). *Apprenticeship in thinking: Cognitive development in social context.* Oxford, England: Oxford University Press.

Rohrkemper, M., & Corno, L. (1988). Success and failure on classroom tasks: Adaptive learning and classroom teaching. *Elementary School Journal, 88,* 297–312.

Stevenson, H. W., & Stigler, J. (1992). *The learning gap.* New York: Summit Books.

Stipek, D. J. (1993). *Motivation to learn: From theory to practice.* Boston: Allyn & Bacon.

Stipek, D. J., & MacIver, D. (1989). Developmental change in children's assessment of intellectual competence. *Child Development, 60,* 521–538.

Tharp, R. G., & Gallimore, R. (1988). *Rousing minds to life: Teaching, learning, and schooling in social context.* Cambridge, England: Cambridge University Press.

Tierney, R. J., Carter, M. A., & Desai, L. E. (1991). *Portfolio assessment in the reading-writing classroom.* Norwood, MA: Christopher-Gordon.

Towler, L., & Broadfoot, P. (1992). Self-assessment in the primary school. *Educational Review, 44,* 137–151.

Valencia, S. W., (1990). Alternative assessment: Separating the wheat from the chaff. *The Reading Teacher, 44,* 60–61.

Valencia, S. W., Hiebert, E. H., & Afflerbach, P. P. (1994). *Authentic reading assessment: Practices and possibilities.* Newark, DE: International Reading Association.

Valencia, S., & Pearson, P. D. (1987). Reading assessment: A time for change. *The Reading Teacher, 40,* 726–733.

van Kraayenoord, C. E. (1993, December). Toward self-assessment of literacy learning. Keynote address to the International Reading Association, San Antonio, Texas.

van Kraayenoord, C. E., & Paris, S. G. (1992). Portfolio assessment: Its place in the Australian classroom. *Australian Journal of Language and Literacy, 15,* 93–104.

Vygotsky, L. S. (1978). *Mind in society.* Cambridge, MA: Harvard University Press.

Weeks, B., & Leaker, J. (1991). *Managing literacy assessment with young learners.* Evanston, IL: McDougal, Littell & Co.

Weiner, B. (1992). *Human motivation: Metaphors, theories, and research.* Newbury Park, CA: Sage.

Winograd, P., Paris, S., & Bridge, C. (1991). Improving the assessment of reading. *The Reading Teacher, 45,* 108–116.

Wolf, D., Bixby, J., Glenn, J., & Gardner, H. (1991). To use their minds well: Investigating new forms of student assessment. In G. Grant (Ed.), *Review of Research in Education* (Vol. 17, pp. 31–74). New York: American Educational Research Association.

Zimmerman, B. J. (1989). Models of self-regulated learning and academic achievement. In B. Zimmerman & D. Schunk (Eds.), *Self-regulated learning and academic achievement: Theory, research, and practice* (pp. 1–25). New York: Springer-Verlag.

ABOUT THE AUTHORS

Scott G. Paris is a professor of psychology and education at the University of Michigan, his undergraduate alma mater. He received his PhD from Indiana University and has studied children's learning, literacy, and motivation with a variety of methods for more than 20 years. His work with children and educators in Australia, as well as across America, has provided valuable opportunities to learn about different approaches to education. His research extends and applies theories from developmental and educational psychology to practical problems of learning and instruction in K–12 classrooms.

Linda R. Ayres is the language arts coordinator for Walled Lake Consolidated Schools in Michigan. She was an elementary school teacher and reading specialist and has participated in children's literacy education at many levels. She completed her PhD in reading and language arts at Oakland University, where her research focused on young children's phonological awareness and reading acquisition. Other interests include reading comprehension, writing instruction, and cross-age tutoring. Linda and Scott have collaborated for several years on the portfolio project described in this book.